Educate and Survive

A compilation of Survival Knowledge

Micah L. McGuire

ISBN-13:978-1545130551
ISBN-10:1545130558

Table of Contents

Educate and Survive

A compilation of Survival Knowledge

By U.S. Army Veteran Micah L. McGuire

Published by Micah L. McGuire

Formatted by eBooksMade4You@gmail.com

Author's Note

This is a collection of tips, advice, and instructions I have found in my own research and experience. Multiple unknown sources may have been quoted in this book. This is an attempt to compile a survival guide to help keep you alive if and when the need arises.

A word to the wise

One thing you don't want to be during a catastrophic event is dependent on the system. The more you can take care of yourself, the better off you'll be physically, financially, emotionally and even spiritually. Here are 20 suggestions to prepare you for what may come (If you're able to).

Get a small solar system that can be used to run a laptop or recharge batteries

Drill a water well and install a hand pump or solar-powered DC pump

Set up a rainwater collection system from your own home

Stash some money, mostly coins and gold if possible

Own and learn how to use a handgun, rifle and shotgun

Store as much ammunition as possible

Own and know how to use a water filter

Start a garden this spring and acquire more food production skills

Save garden seeds so you can plant the next generation of food

Acquire a wood-burning stove for heat and cooking

Possess a large quantity of stored food

Store up valuable barter items that are relatively cheap today: Alcohol, coffee, ammo, matches, etc.

Safely store extra vehicle fuel (gasoline, diesel) at your home or ranch. Be sure to use fuel stabilizers to extend their life.

Learn emergency first aid skills and own first aid supplies. This could save a life or possibly save a trip to the emergency room.

Start growing your own medicinal plants and grow aloe vera, oregano, garlic, cayenne pepper and other medicinal herbs that can replace a surprisingly large number of prescription drugs. Oregano, for example, is a potent antibiotic. Aloe vera treats cuts, scrapes and burns.

Boost your immune system with vitamin D and superfoods

Increase your level of physical fitness

Learn how to raise animals such as rabbits, chickens, goats or cows.

Educate Yourself! Your plan C is education, skills, and knowledge.

Take a Free CPR course through the American Red Cross as well as learn the Heimlich Maneuver.

Knowledge is power, so if you want to get smart try learning Human Anatomy and Physiology, Veterinary Medicine, EMT, Intermediate and Paramedic skills, Automotive, Metal Working, Aquaponics, Solar Energy Guides, Wind Turbine Guides, Composting, Homesteading, and one that many preppers overlook - "Ocean Water Distillation" (making ocean water drinkable and usable on crops).

Collect storage items such as an extra bag of rice, dried beans, oats, and legumes.

Buy powdered milk, and SALT (salt is valuable for various reasons including curing meats to last longer).

Here are some tips to start setting items aside:

Weekly:

> 1 case of bottled Water
> 1 or 2 rolls of toilet paper
> 1 roll of paper towels
> 1 package of napkins
> 1 bag rice
> 1 bag dried pinto beans
> 1 bag lentils
>
> 4 to 6 extra canned goods (canned tuna in OIL, canned chicken, spam, canned ham, soups, fruits, vegetables, etc.)
>
> Buying in bulk is cheaper in the long run. Freeze bags of rice for 3 days, pack them in clean sterile mason jars with BAY LEAVES and "Oven Can" them. Rice weevil's dislike bay leaves!

Bi-Monthly

> bars of soap
> freeze dried anything
> laundry soap
> textbooks
> Peroxide
> Rubbing Alcohol
> baby wipes

Monthly

> Package of unscented Tampons. You can use these for the obvious reasons or even stop wounds or start fires. No woman wants to be without these.
>
> Ketchup
> Spices

Alcohol bottles and packs of cigarettes for bartering
shampoo and conditioner
Candles
distilled white vinegar
batteries
bleach

Security

Security is no laughing matter. If you ignore this you will lose all you've worked for and possibly your life. It's important to remember you are still human when dealing with outsiders, but never be too quick to trust.

Start by making sure all your additions to your living place and storage areas are secure in that they are not easy targets for less fortunate neighbors.

Know your area: Be aware of your surroundings and take care of yourself and your loved ones by keeping calm through tough times. It's important not to lose your head and learn from all your experiences. Know where your attacks may come from and take care to minimize them. Know where you can restock on water and food as well as medical supplies, if possible.

Camouflage: Disguise what you have built if possible. Build under heavy tree coverage or even underground, provided it is not a flood friendly area. Being seen can be good if you're expecting help to come, but if your focus is to be hidden you should also consider light and noise discipline as well as who you confide in.

Fortitude: Secure all possible entrances in and out without blocking any chance of escape during fire. If possible secure your loved ones and yourself in a dwelling that's not easily penetrated or easy to burn down.

Location: Low lying areas are good for not being seen, but a higher elevation will give you an advantage point against an oncoming attack. Be sure to consider weather elements and escape routes.

Defense: Booby traps are pretty much illegal in todays civilized world, but in case of a total society fallout, you might want to get creative. Body armor, gas masks and weapons might be a very wise investment.

Intelligent Investments

Save up your change! Gold is a precious medal now and always was; safe to say it always will be.

Water - The most important intelligent investment; you cannot survive without it. If you can gather and filter your own you will be a lot better off.

Food - It's quite easy to buy a few items weekly, bi-monthly, and monthly. Adding a few items at a time is an easy way to save while you still can

Medical Supplies and Antibiotics

Get a medical kit and ensure it has these following items:

- Instant heating pads
- Emergency dental kit
- Alcohol
- Peroxide
- Irrigation syringes
- Blood clotting packs
- Scalpel
- Forceps
- Long Tweezers
- Bent snips
- Nasopharyngeal airway
- Chest seal (HALO)
- Battle Dressing
- Tourniquet
- Sterile Gauze in various sizes
- Liquid skin
- Pocket resuscitator

Weapons and other items to collect

It would be wise to buy and learn how to disassemble and reassemble your gun(s) for cleaning – after purchase make sure to buy ammunition.

It would be wise to purchase items not requiring the purchase of ammunition like sling shots with ball bearings, bows and arrows, crossbows and blowguns. As farfetched as it may sound you can hunt with these.

Make thrift stores a part of your weekly shopping; you can find lots of useful items cheap! Mason jars, oil lamps, wool and denim clothing and fleece blankets, tents, wagons, rain gear, cast iron pots and pans, silver utensils, old fashioned hand powered kitchen utensils/appliances. and many, many, other important items.

Bugout bag
(contents)

1. Knives
2. Slingshot
3. Wire saw
4. Trade items
5. Arrowheads
6. Fishing tackle
7. Hand sanitizer
8. Batteries
9. Flashlight (L.E.D. and extra bulbs)
10. Gloves
11. Wet weather gear
12. Spare pants/shirts (different colors)
13. First aid kit
14. Hatchet
15. e-tool (folding shovel)
16. Hand gun and ammo
17. Char cloth
18. Compass
19. Sewing kit
20. Medicine (stomach sickness, pain, fever, allergy)
21. Toilet paper
22. Matches, lighter, striker
23. String, 550 cord, rope, bungee
24. Duct tape
25. Water purification tablets
26. Signal mirror

What are the symptoms of dehydration?

Mild to moderate dehydration is likely to cause:
> Dry, sticky mouth
> Sleepiness or tiredness — children are likely to be less active than usual
> Increased thirst
> Dry mouth and swollen tongue...
> Lethargy or coma (with severe dehydration)
> Low or no urine output; urine looks dark yellow
> No tears
> Dizziness
> Headache
> Confusion

If a person is asking for water and has these symptoms, give them shade, water, and loosen all tight laces and belts. If the person has already blacked out, seek medical attention or at least an IV.

Water filtering

1. You need two buckets stacked on each other
2. Poke a hole in bottom of top bucket, fill bucket with sand (to remove debris and bacteria)
3. Put holes in top and bottom of bottom bucket, fill with crushed charcoal
4. Water coming out will be cloudy, if possible use a coffee filter
5. It is very important to boil the water to remove any remaining bacteria and prevent stomach sickness and diarrhea.

Water Pumps

Solar Water Pumps, Solar Pump Systems, DC Powered Water Pumps

It may be important to pump your stored water. Here is a picture I found that may be easy to replicate.

How to make snake Anti-venom

*This can be extremely dangerous and is not something that should be attempted by amateurs or the inexperienced:

Step 1: Milking the Venom

The first step is getting your hands on a lot of snakes, which are quarantined and monitored for weeks to months to ensure their good health. Before milking, put on protective gloves. Famed snake handler Bill Haast used his bare hands, but was eventually bitten on the right index finger, rendering him unable to wrangle serpents – his lifelong passion. Move the snake into a clean milking room. With some of the most deadly snakes, like banded kraits or black mambas, experts often use a short-acting anesthetic to calm the snake down.

Next, grab the snake with the thumb and index finger at the very back of the head, just behind the angle of the jaw where the venom glands reside. This allows you to press on the glands while preventing the snake from turning its head and striking you. Opening a snake's jaws may require gentle pressure, and with vipers, you might have to use forceps to swivel their fangs into the upright position and pull back the sheath covering the fang's hollow tip.

Take a vial and cover it with a rubber or plastic film. Then, snake in hand, push the fangs through the plastic (or let the snake simply strike on its own). Gently squeeze the glands to get out all the venom. In some cases, anti-venom makers use a weak electric current to stimulate venom excretion. Carefully remove the fangs from the film. Snakes with fangs in the back of their mouths, such as colubrids, may require special tubes to bite into, which drain into a collection vial.

To get enough venom, each snake must be milked many times. For example, in 1965, the National Institutes of Health asked Haast, who founded the Miami Serpentarium, to produce 1 pint of coral snake venom. It took him, a man of unrivaled skill and patience, a total of three years and 69,000 milkings to get that much, from which the first and only American coral anti-venom was made. Wyeth (now owned by Pfizer) produced this same anti-venom until 2003, when it closed the factory. Since then the FDA–which must approve anti-venom the same way it approves other drugs – has extended the expiration date of the scant remaining supplies three times because the supply threatens to run out soon.

Step 2: Cooling Down and Labeling

Once milked, the venom must be cooled to below minus 20 Celsius and usually freeze-dried for easier storage and transport. Freeze-drying concentrates the venom and removes the water. It's important to clearly label the venom with the snake's species, any relevant subspecies and geographical origin, since venom can vary wildly between members of the same species, especially between young and old snakes (older ones are more venomous).

Step 3: Choosing an Animal for Immunization

Horses are most commonly chosen as the animals to create antibodies because they thrive in many environments worldwide, have a large body mass, get along with each other and are forgiving. "When they see you coming at them with a needle two to three times, they don't attack you," Boyer says. "They're friendly animals with big veins and they have long lives." Goats and sheep can work well, too. People have also used donkeys, rabbits, cats, chickens, camels, rodents and even sharks. "Sharks make nice antibodies," Boyer says, "but obviously aren't easy to work with."

Step 4: Immunizing

Prep the venom for injection by carefully measuring it out and mixing it with distilled water or a buffer solution. Then mix in some kind of adjuvant–a chemical that causes the horse's immune system to react and produce antibodies that bind to and neutralize the venom.

Inject a small amount (say a few milliliters) of the solution beneath the horse's skin, preferably on its rump or the back of its neck where lymph nodes and immune cells reside. It's usually a good idea to break up the shot into smaller doses in various locations to avoid causing an ulcer or sore on the skin and to maximize the surface area for an immune reaction. This part of the process can vary depending upon the type of anti-venom, the company involved, the snake used and the sort of antibodies desired.

The specific details are hush-hush. "These are closely guarded trade secrets by people who make anti-venom worldwide – how much venom is administered in what fashion to get an immune response," Boyer says.

It's vital to have a trained veterinarian on hand to monitor the horse's health. If it tolerates the injection, you'll probably give it several more doses days or weeks apart. Antibodies in the horse's bloodstream peak after about eight to 10 weeks. At that point the horse is ready to be bled, which involves drawing 3 to 6 liters of blood from the jugular vein, according to WHO guidelines.

Step 5: Purifying

Use a centrifuge to filter the plasma, the liquid portion of the blood not including blood cells. The WHO recommends injecting the blood cells back into the horse, although horses can usually stay alive and healthy without this.

Now it's time to separate out the anti-venom. Again, this multistep process varies by anti-venom producer. Generally, it begins by getting rid of unwanted proteins. You do this by causing them to precipitate, or fall out, often by adjusting the plasma's pH or adding salts to the solution.

One of the last steps involves using an enzyme to break down the antibody into small parts and isolating its active ingredient. In the case of CroFab, the only FDA-licensed anti-venom produced in the U.S. (which treats bites from all North American species except the coral snake), the sheep-derived antibodies are digested with the enzyme papain. Alvin Bronstein, medical director of the Rocky Mountain Poison Center, says this creates a small antibody with a much lower likelihood of causing an allergic reaction compared to its predecessor. "It's a revolutionary treatment for snakebite," he says.

Step 6: Human Use

Once approved, the purified antibody product is freeze-dried or concentrated into powder or liquid form and put into vials for shipment. The anti-venom usually needs to be refrigerated or frozen, which further hinders storing for long periods of time if electricity is no longer available or may be unreliable. Once the product reaches an emergency room and a snakebite victim arrives, the vials are usually filled with saline solution and injected intravenously. If everything goes right, the antibodies then bind to and neutralize the venom, while the liver or kidneys clear out the excess chemicals.

Mosquito repellant

Ingredients:
1/2 liter of alcohol

100 grams of whole cloves

100 ml of baby oil or similar (almond, sesame, chamomile, lavender, fennel, etc.)

Preparation:

Leave cloves to marinate in alcohol four days

Stir every morning and evening

After 4 days add the oil

It's now ready to use.

How to use:

Gently rub a few drops into the skin of the arms and legs.

Observe the mosquitoes fleeing the room.

Repels fleas on pets too.

Lemons and their uses

1. Lemons freshen the Fridge

   Remove refrigerator odors with ease. Dab lemon juice on a cotton ball or sponge and leave it in the fridge for several hours. Make sure to toss out any malodorous items that might be causing the bad smell.

2. High Blood Pressure

   Lemon contains potassium which controls high blood pressure and reduces the effect of nausea and dizziness.

3. Prevent Cauliflower from Turning Brown

   Cauliflower tends to turn brown with even the slightest cooking. You can make sure the white vegetables stay white by squeezing a teaspoon of fresh lemon juice on them before heating.

4. Mental Health

   Lemon water can also prep up your mood and relieve you from depression and stress.

5. Refresh Cutting Boards

   No wonder your kitchen cutting board smells! After all, you use it to chop onions, crush garlic, and prepare fish. To get rid of the smell and help sanitize the cutting board, rub it all over with the cut side of half a lemon or wash it in undiluted juice straight from the bottle.

6. Respiratory Problems

   Lemon water can reduce phlegm and can also help you breathe properly and aids a person suffering with asthma.

7. Treating Arthritis and Rheumatism

Lemon is a diuretic — assists in the production of urine which helps you to reduce inflammation by flushing out toxins and bacteria while also giving you relief from arthritis and rheumatism.

8. Prevents Kidney Stones

Regular consumption of the refreshing drink — or even lemon juice mixed with water — may increase the production of urinary citrate, a chemical in the urine that prevents the formation of crystals that may build up into kidney stones.

9. Keep Insects Out of the Kitchen

You don't need insecticides or ant traps to ant-proof your kitchen. Just give it the lemon treatment. First squirt some lemon juice on door thresholds and windowsills. Then squeeze lemon juice into any holes or cracks where the ants may be getting in. Finally, scatter small slices of lemon peel around the outdoor entrance. The ants will get the message that they aren't welcome. Lemons are also effective against roaches and fleas: Simply mix the juice of 4 lemons (along with the rinds) with 1/2 gallon (2 liters) water and wash your floors with it; then watch the fleas and roaches flee. They hate the smell.

10. Anti-Aging

Lemon water reduces the production of free radicals which are responsible for aging skin and skin damage. Lemon water is calorie free and an antioxidant.

11. Fruit and Vegetable Wash

You never know what kind of pesticides or dirt may be lurking on the skin of your favorite fruits and vegetables. Slice your lemon and squeeze out one tablespoon of lemon juice into your spray bottle. The lemon juice is a natural disinfectant and will leave your fruits and vegetables smelling nice too.

12. Treat Infections

Lemon water can fight throat infections thanks to its antibacterial property. If salt water does not work for you, try lime and water for gargling.

13. Deodorize Your Garbage

If your garbage is beginning to smell yucky, here's an easy way to deodorize it: Save leftover lemon and orange peels and toss them at the base under the bag. To keep it smelling fresh, repeat once every couple of weeks.

14. Keep Guacamole Green

You've been making guacamole all day long for the big party, and you don't want it to turn brown on top before the guests arrive. The solution: Sprinkle a liberal amount of fresh lemon juice over it and it will stay fresh and green. The flavor of the lemon juice is a natural complement to the avocados in the guacamole. Make the fruit salad hours in advance, too. Just squeeze some lemon juice onto the apple slices, and they'll stay snowy white.

15. Purges the Blood

We consume a lot of junk food or food with a lot of preservatives and artificial flavors. This builds up a lot of toxins in the blood and body, but daily consumption of lemon water helps to purify the blood.

16. Make Soggy Lettuce Crisp

Don't toss that soggy lettuce into the garbage. With the help of a little lemon juice you can toss it in a salad instead. Add the juice of half a lemon to a bowl of cold water. Then put the soggy lettuce in it and refrigerate for 1 hour. Make sure to dry the leaves completely before putting them into salads or sandwiches.

17. Oral Health

Lemon juice also stops bleeding gums and reduces toothaches

18. Lighten Age Spots

Why buy expensive creams when you've got lemon juice? To lighten liver spots or freckles, try applying lemon juice directly to the area. Let it sit for 15 minutes and then rinse your skin clean. It's a safe and effective skin-lightening agent.

19. Create Blonde Highlights

For salon-worthy highlights, add 1/4 cup lemon juice to 3/4 cup water and rinse your hair with the mixture. Then sit in the sun until your hair dries. To maximize the effect, repeat once daily for up to a week.

20. Make a Room Scent/Humidifier

Freshen and moisturize the air in your home on dry winter days. Make your own room scent that also doubles as a humidifier. If you have a wood-burning stove, place an enameled cast-iron pot or bowl on top, fill with water, and add lemon (and/or orange) peels, cinnamon sticks, cloves, and apple skins. No wood-burning stove? Use your stovetop instead and just simmer the water periodically.

21. Clean and Whiten Nails

Pamper your hands without a manicurist. Add the juice of 1/2 lemon to 1 cup warm water and soak your fingertips in the mixture for 5 minutes. After pushing back the cuticles, rub some lemon peel back and forth against the nail.

22. Cleanse Your Face

Zap zits naturally by dabbing lemon juice on blackheads to draw them out during the day. You can also wash your face with lemon juice for a natural cleanse and exfoliation. Your skin should improve after several days of treatment. Lemon water is also a cooling agent, best way to beat the heat.

23. Freshen Your Breath

Make an impromptu mouthwash by rinsing with lemon juice straight from the bottle. Swallow for longer-lasting fresh breath. The citric acid in the juice alters the pH level in your mouth, killing bacteria that cause bad breath. Rinse after a few minutes because long-term exposure to the acid in lemons can harm tooth enamel.

24. Treat Flaky Dandruff

If itchy, scaly dandruff has you scratching your head, relief may be no farther away than your refrigerator. Just massage two tablespoons lemon juice into your scalp and rinse with water. Then stir one teaspoon lemon juice into one cup water and rinse your hair with it. Repeat daily until your dandruff disappears.

25. Get Rid of Tough Stains on Marble

You probably think of marble as stone, but it is really petrified calcium (also known as old seashells). That explains why it is so porous and easily stained and damaged. Those stains can be hard to remove. If washing won't remove a stubborn stain, try this: Cut a lemon in half, dip the exposed flesh into some table salt, and rub it vigorously on the stain. But do this only as a last resort; acid can damage marble. Rinse well. Use These Lemons to Clean – Easy and Effective

26. Remove Berry Stains

It sure was fun to pick your own berries, but now your fingers are stained with berry juice that won't come off no matter how much you scrub with soap and water. Try washing your hands with undiluted lemon juice, then wait a few minutes and wash with warm, soapy water. Repeat until your hands are stain-free.

27. Soften Dry, Scaly Elbows

Itchy elbows are bad enough, but they look terrible too. For better looking (and feeling) elbows, mix baking soda and lemon juice to make an abrasive paste, then rub it into your elbows for a soothing, smoothing, and exfoliating treatment. Rinse your extremities in a mixture of equal parts lemon juice and water, then massage with olive oil and dab dry with a soft cloth.

28. Headaches

Lemon juice with a few teaspoons of hot tea added is the treatment of a sophisticated New York bartender, for those who suffer with hangover headaches– and from headaches due to many other causes. He converts his customers to this regime, and weans them away from drug remedies completely.

29. Chills and Fevers

Chills and fevers may be due to a variety of causes; never the less the lemon is always a helpful remedy. Spanish physicians regard it as an infallible friend.

30. Diphtheria

Skip the vaccine for this disease. Lemon Juice Treatment still proves as one of the most powerful antiseptics and the strong digestive qualities of the fruit are admired around the world. With the juice every hour or two, and at the same time, 1/2 to 1 tsp. should be swallowed. This cuts loose the false membrane in the throat and permits it to come out.

31. Vaginal Hygiene

Diluted lemon juice makes a safe and sane method of vaginal hygiene. Though it is a powerful antiseptic it is nevertheless free from irritating drugs in douches and suppositories.

32. Forget the Moth Balls

A charming French custom to keep closets free from moths is to take ripe lemons and stick them with cloves all over the skin. The heavily studded lemons slowly dry with their cloves, leaving a marvelous odor throughout the closets and rooms.

33. Stomach Health

Digestive problems are the most common ailments but warm water and lime juice is the solution to most digestive problems. Lemon juice helps to purify the blood, reduces your chances of indigestion, constipation, eliminates toxins from the body, adds digestion and reduces phlegm.

34. Disinfect Cuts and Scrapes

Stop bleeding and disinfect minor cuts and scrapes by pouring a few drops of lemon juice directly on the cut. You can also apply the juice with a cotton ball and hold firmly in place for one minute.

35. Soothe Poison Ivy Rash

You won't need an ocean of calamine lotion the next time poison ivy comes a-creeping. Just apply lemon juice directly to the affected area to soothe itching and alleviate the rash.

36. Remove Warts

You've tried countless remedies to banish warts and nothing seems to work. Next time, apply a dab of lemon juice directly to the wart using a cotton swab. Repeat for several days until the acids in the lemon juice dissolve the wart completely.

37. Bleach Delicate Fabrics

Avoid additional bleach stains by swapping ordinary household chlorine bleach with lemon juice, which is milder but no less effective. Soak your delicates in a mixture of lemon juice and baking soda for at least half an hour before washing.

38. Clean Tarnished Brass and Polish Chrome

Say good-bye to tarnish on brass, copper, or stainless steel. Make a paste of lemon juice and salt (or substitute baking soda or cream of tartar for the salt) and coat the affected area. Let it stay on for 5 minutes. Then wash in warm water, rinse, and polish dry. Use the same mixture to clean metal kitchen sinks too. Apply the paste, scrub gently, and rinse. Get rid of mineral deposits and polish chrome faucets and other tarnished chrome. Simply rub lemon rind over the chrome and watch it shine! Rinse well and dry with a soft cloth.

39. Replace Your Dry Cleaner

Ditch the expensive dry-cleaning bills (and harsh chemicals) with this homegrown trick. Simply scrub the stained area on shirts and blouses with equal parts lemon juice and water. Your "pits" will be good as new, and smell nice too.

40. Boost Laundry Detergent

For more powerful cleaning action, pour 1 cup lemon juice into the washer during the wash cycle. The natural bleaching action of the juice will zap stains and remove rust and mineral discolorations from cotton T-shirts and briefs and will leave your clothes smelling fresh. Your clothes will turn out brighter and also come out smelling lemon-fresh.

41. Rid Clothes of Mildew

Have you ever unpacked clothes you stored all winter and discovered some are stained with mildew? To get rid of it, make a paste of lemon juice and salt and rub it on the affected area, then dry the clothes in sunlight. Repeat the process until the stain is gone.

42. Eliminate Fireplace Odor

There's nothing cozier on a cold winter night than a warm fire burning in the fireplace â€" unless the fire happens to smell horrible. Next time you have a fire that sends a stench into the room, try throwing a few lemon peels into the flames. Or simply burn some lemon peels along with your firewood as a preventive measure.

43. Neutralize Cat-Box Odor

You don't have to use an aerosol spray to neutralize foul-smelling cat-box odors or freshen the air in your bathroom. Just cut a couple of lemons in half. Then place them, cut side up, in a dish in the room, and the air will soon smell lemon-fresh.

44. Deodorize a Humidifier

When your humidifier starts to smell funky, deodorize it with ease: Just pour 3 or 4 teaspoons lemon juice into the water. It will not only remove the off odor but will replace it with a lemon-fresh fragrance. Repeat every couple of weeks to keep the odor from returning.

45. Reduce Asthma Symptoms

In addition to a general detoxifying diet, 2 tablespoons of lemon juice before each meal, and before retiring can reduce asthma symptoms.
Cherries help with muscle cramps and inflammation
Spinach, garlic and bell peppers can be used as antibiotics

OMELET IN A BAG

INGREDIENTS:

Eggs – About 2-3 eggs per person
Mix-Ins – Cheese, Bell Pepper, Onion, Bacon, Tomatoes, Ham, etc…
Bags – Get bags you can boil food in

Toppings – Salsa, Cheese, etc…

Put 2-3 eggs and whatever you want in your omelet in the bag. Mix it all together and put the bags into a pot of boiling water. Boil it for 10-12 minutes and then remove the bags from the water. Dump your omelet in a bowl, or just eat it straight out of the bag! Add any desired toppings!

Bow Drill Set

Bow Drill Set 1 - Making the Set

One of the most key rules when it comes to making a functional bow drill set is choosing wood that is dry. Don't use anything that is lying on the ground.

The second key part to your bow drill is choosing wood for your spindle and hearth that is of a medium-density. Cedar, cottonwood, basswood, and willow are ideal for creating your set. Your hearth piece will need to be about 12 to 14 inches long. The spindle will need to be about 6 to 8 inches in length.

Your handhold piece needs to be out of hardwood or even a rock. Your bow piece should be about arm's length. Beech trees are perfect for making a bow. Now for cordage, you will generally find that paracord is best. Although it is possible to use natural cordage, it can be extremely difficult. For training purposes, it is best to use man-made cordage.

Bow Drill Set 2 - Fine Tuning the Set

Making a fire with a bow drill is certainly not a new skill nor is it completely obsolete. You will find plenty of folks who have been kind enough to post videos on YouTube detailing the fine art of fire making. However, if you pay close attention, you will note there is one crucial step missing--the fine tuning. You cannot simply grab a few branches and make a bow drill and expect fire to happen. There are some tweaks that will need to be made.

Hand Hold

- Hard wood, rock or even a metal cap would work for this piece
- A dimple cut in middle of hand hold should allow spindle to turn freely.
- Lubrication for spindle can be ear wax, oil from your skin, green acorns or…snot.

Spindle

- Needs to be about 6 to 8 inches or "Aloha" length between your pinkie and thumb
- Hand hold end should be pointed.

- End that fits into hearth should be rounded.
- Smooth sides that are not too rough or bumpy.
- Thickness should be about as big as your thumb

Hearth or Fireboard

- About 12 to 14 inches long, or comfortable enough for you to stand on one side
- Thickness of your thumb.
- The pie piece (where the spark starts) should be about 1/7 to 1/8 of the circle.
- The pie piece should extend into the middle of the burn hole.

Bow

- Length should extend from about your armpit to the tip of your fingers.
- Width will vary depending on what works best for you.
- Cordage can really be anything. However, when you are first starting, avoid paracord or other material that has a sheen on it. This makes the fire starting process super easy.

Bow Drill Set 3 - Working the Set

Probably one of the most misleading aspects of all those videos on YouTube or clips you see in the movies about fire making is how easy it is. It takes a lot of practice to learn the art of starting a fire without matches or other convenient tools. However, once you do figure out how to do it, you will do just fine. The following are a few more tips to help you get started in learning the skill of bow drill fire making.

- Place your non-dominant foot (if you are right-handed this would be your left leg) as close to the spindle as possible, but don't get in the way of the spindle.
- Put your dominant knee behind the other foot.
- Lean forward and wrap your arm around your leg. This will help use your core body strength and not solely rely on your arm for the spinning motion.
- Place enough pressure on your hand hold to keep it upright, but don't put too much and prevent it from spinning freely.
- Keep the spindle straight up and down.
- Your spindle will be on the outside of your cordage.
- Start out slow. Those first few turns are done to create a little dust.
- Once the pie piece starts to fill up with dust, then start cranking up the spinning motion.
- Use the whole bow in the action.

Troubleshooting

- If the dust is not a dark brown, apply more pressure to the hand hold.

- Your cord should remain firm on the spindle, if it does, tighten it up a bit. If the spindle is not moving freely, your string is probably too tight and needs to be loosened a bit.

- If the spindle goes flying, relax, and try again with it at a 90 degree angle. You could also cut bigger dimples.

- If you see lots of good dust, but no spark, get a closer look. Do not do this in direct sunlight--you will not be able to see those first embers.

- You wear out before you get that first coal. Well, you need to get in better shape. Follow these tips and you will get that first ember.

21 HOME REMEDIES FOR A TOOTHACHE

Anyone who has ever had the misfortune of a toothache knows that it is not just your mouth that hurts. A toothache can be felt in just about every part of your body.

Although in most cases only a doctor can cure the source of the problem, this list of treatments and pain relief remedies should get you through until you can visit the dentist.

Directions: Apply the below remedies directly to both the problem tooth and surrounding gums unless otherwise directed.

For items that direct you to chew, or for liquids that are to be swished around inside mouth, direct the liquid on and around the sore tooth as much as possible.

Do not swallow liquids. Rinse your mouth and spit them out when done.

1. Salt Water: Mix a heaping tablespoon full of salt in a small glass of warm water; swirl around inside your mouth for as long as you can, spit out. Repeat as needed.

2. Hydrogen Peroxide: Swoosh a bit of hydrogen peroxide. If the taste is too horrid for you, try diluting with a bit of water. Hydrogen peroxide will tend to foam in your mouth.

3. Alcohol: Swoosh a bit of whiskey, scotch, brandy or vodka. A strong mouthwash that contains alcohol will do the trick, too.

4. Vanilla Extract: Saturate a cotton ball with vanilla and hold in place. Can also use a cotton swab dipped in extract. Other extracts that have the same effect are:

   Almond Extract
   Peppermint Extract
   Lemon Extract

5. Tea Tree Oil: Just a drop or two will do the trick. You can also add some to a cotton swab and hold in place or add a few drops of tea tree oil to a small glass of lukewarm to warm water and rinse your mouth with it.

6. Oil of Oregano: Mix a few drops with a bit of olive oil, then saturate a cotton ball with mixture. Can replace the olive oil with lukewarm water if preferred.

7. Apple Cider Vinegar: Soak a cotton ball with apple cider vinegar (ACV) and hold it in place. Can also try regular household vinegar.

8. Ginger Root: Take a fresh piece of ginger and chew it a bit.

9. Garlic: Take a clove of garlic, smash it and apply (settle it inside cheek). You can also mash some garlic with salt.

10. Peppermint Leaves: Chew on fresh peppermint leaves. You can also use dried leaves; just hold them in place.

11. Potato: Cut a fresh piece of potato (raw, skin off) and hold in place. Can also pound a piece of raw potato, mix in a bit of salt and use the mash.

12. Lime: Cut a slice or wedge of lime and apply, bite into it if you can to release some of the juice.

13. Onion: Slice a piece of fresh onion and hold it inside your mouth. The onion needs to be freshly cut (so it provides a bit of onion juice).

14. Plantain: Chew up a fresh plantain leaf. If you're too sore to chew, use the other side of your mouth. Once the leaf is macerated a bit apply it to the problem area and hold in place.

15. Cucumber: Slice a fresh piece of cucumber and hold it over the sore area. If refrigerated, you might want to bring the cucumber to room temperature before using (if sensitive to cold) otherwise a cool piece can be soothing. You can also mash a piece with a bit of salt and pack it around the sore tooth.

16. Cayenne Pepper: Make a paste with cayenne pepper and water.

17. Black Pepper: You can use this full strength or make a mix of pepper and salt.

18. Baking Soda: Take a cotton swab and moisten it with a bit of water, dip it in baking soda (coat the swab really well with baking soda) then apply. You can also make a mouth rinse by mixing a heaping spoonful of baking soda in a small glass of lukewarm to warm water, dissolve the soda then swish the mixture in your mouth.

19. Cloves: This is remedy from the old timers (my great grandparents era), rest a clove against the sore area until pain goes away. You can also use a drop or two of clove oil (BE CAREFUL: too much can be toxic) or make a thick paste of ground cloves and water or ground cloves and olive oil.

20. Tea: Make a fresh cup of tea then take the used tea bag (still warm) and stick it in

your mouth. Careful not to tear the bag. The tannins that are naturally in tea leaves can help numb things.

21. Ice Pack: Cover an ice pack with a face cloth or towel then hold over your cheek where the problem is. This will help numb things. Make sure that you have some type of cloth between your skin and the ice, otherwise you can severely damage your skin. If that doesn't work, try the opposite–a hot compress (making sure that it is not so hot as to scald your skin).

Tips

If the pain is unbearable and there's no dentist available, call your local hospital's emergency room–chances are they have a dentist on call that can treat you (for a fee of course).

Try gently brushing your teeth and flossing–this might bring some relief.

One old time remedy that you should not follow is to place an aspirin against the sore tooth. You will have just as much if not more of an effect by swallowing the aspirin. Aspirin is actually an acid (acetylsalicylic acid to be exact) and placing it directly against your gums or teeth will cause corrosion of your teeth and acid burns on your gums.

If the side of your face is in severe pain and it feels like you're going to lose your mind (I've been there, done that)–it could be a sinus infection or an allergy that affects your sinuses rather than a problem tooth (even though it definitely feels like it). Try taking a decongestant or if that is not available, a shower set on the hottest setting may help clear your sinus cavities.

Please be aware: These are notes I have collected from research. They are not by any means professional medical advice.

Saving seeds

Saving seeds to use for the next year's garden is not difficult once you understand the process. As more people turn to gardening to supplement their food source, saving seeds is a great way to save money and eat healthier.

The following is a step by step guide to saving seeds for beginners.

Selecting the Plants

The process starts by selecting the best plants from which to gather seeds. Some plants are easier to harvest seeds from than others. Lettuce, peas, peppers, beans, and tomatoes are all good choices for beginners.

These plants each have self-pollinating flowers. This means that the seeds from these plants will need very little treatment before they are stored. Seeds from self-pollinated plants will also produce plants exactly like the parent plants.

Eggplant and Endive also produce seeds that are self-pollinated.

Many plants have male and female flower parts. Making sure that the pollination process is not contaminated is trickier. Some plants are also pollinated by the wind or insects.

Melons, pumpkins, and cucumbers can be cross-pollinated by insects and are also more difficult for beginners. Selecting seeds from hybrid plants may work, but the new plants will not be exactly the same as the old ones.

The new plant will be a new combination of various good and bad traits from the original plant. Whether you plan to save seeds from plants that self-pollinate or not, be sure to select seeds from the best tasting fruits and vegetables.

Harvesting the Seeds

Once the best plants have been selected, the next step is harvesting the seeds. This step must be done at just the right time and in the proper way. The following are instructions for harvesting seeds from a variety of plants.

1. Peppers

Peppers are probably the easiest seeds to save and a good place for beginners to start. When saving pepper seeds wait until the pepper is fully ripe, even a bit wrinkled, before harvesting the seeds.

Cut the pepper in half. The seeds are located on the center stem. Lightly brush the seeds to remove them from the stem. Individually separate each seed before letting them dry.

2. Tomatoes

When saving tomato seeds use seeds only from fully ripe tomatoes. Then make sure to scoop out all the gel and gooey material surrounding the seeds. Put the gooey mixture along with the seeds in a glass container.

Add some water to the container and swirl it around a few times each day. This mixture will ferment in less than a week. The process is complete when the seeds sink to the bottom of the container.

All of the bad seeds and gooey material will stay on top. The seeds can then be rinsed off and left to dry. Rinse the seeds several times to make sure all the residue has been completely washed away.

Place the seeds on a screen or glass plate. It can take several weeks for the seeds to fully dry out. Cucumber seeds must be fermented in the same way to properly prepare them for storage.

3. Beans and Peas

Bean and pea pods should be crusty and brown before harvesting. This means you will harvest beans and peas to save the seeds several weeks after you would harvest them for eating.

Place the seeds on a screen or woven basket. Stir them every few days. When they are completely dry break open each of the pods and store the seeds.

4. Lettuce

Try to save lettuce seeds from a variety of plants. This way you will get diversity in the type of plants you will grow from the seeds the following year.

Some plants are naturally more resistant to excessive rain while others will not survive a rainy season. Some plants are more resistant to excessive sun and heat while others will wilt if it's a very hot summer.

If you save seeds from only one plant and get a very wet or very hot summer you may lose your entire crop. It is essential to save seeds from a variety of lettuce plants and not rely completely on one type.

A stalk will grow from the top of each lettuce plant. This stalk will eventually turn into a flower and self-pollinate. It will then turn into a puff ball similar to what dandelions turn into. It is now time to collect the seeds.

There are several ways to do this. The easiest is to grab the white puffs in your fingers and pull them out. The tiny seeds will be at the end of the puffs. Put the puffs with the seeds at the end in a container.

During the next several days shake the container. When the dried lettuce flower cracks open, the seeds will come out. The seeds are then ready for permanent storage. Keep the container in a cool, dry place.

5. Melon

Keep in mind that several varieties of melons will cross-pollinate. Be sure to plant only one kind of melon in your garden if you're using any for seeds. Pick melons when they are ripe.

Let them sit inside for a day to two, so the seeds can mature further. Spoon out the seeds and wash them in water. Pour melon seeds and water through a screen. Let the seeds dry out on the screen.

A screened in porch is a good place to let the seeds dry. They need to be in a place under a roof and protected from the elements, but still exposed to a little wind.

If they are left to dry inside, keep them in a breezy area with the windows open. Make sure there aren't any mice in the area where the melon seeds are drying. Mice will eat melon seeds.

Storing the Seeds

Make sure the seeds are completely dry or they will most likely rot during storage. Seeds that move easily and don't stick together are usually dry. Heat and humidity will destroy even the best seeds.

Store the seeds in airtight containers. Glass containers are usually best. The seeds may be put in a paper envelope within the glass container. Keep the seeds in a dry, cool area.

One way to keep seeds dry is to put a couple tablespoons of dry milk wrapped in facial tissues in the bottom of the same container as the seeds. It is recommended to replace the dry milk about every six months.

It is also important not to store seeds in areas that may come in contact with sunlight. This means they should not only be stored inside, but in areas away from windows.

There are lots of ways people store their seeds. They can be kept in plastic baggies in the refrigerator. Seeds can also be stored in paper envelopes that are kept in shoe boxes.

If there isn't room in the fridge, storing them in a dry basement is a good idea. Pepper, tomato, and lettuce seeds are extremely small and may need to be kept more carefully than other seeds.

Washed out vitamin or pill bottles are good ways to store these smaller seeds.

Make sure to label each container with the specific name and the dates they were collected. Most seeds will be good for several years if harvested and stored correctly.

Some seeds like onions, chives, and parsley are only good for one year.

Using the Seeds

When you're ready to plant the seeds remove them from the fridge or basement. Allow the entire container to warm to room temperature before removing the seeds.

If the seeds are removed too quickly condensation may cause the seeds to clump together. No matter how well the seeds are stored not all will survive.

Test the quality of your seeds by trying to germinate a few in a moist paper towel. Spread the seeds out evenly and then cover with another damp paper towel.

If the seeds are healthy they should break open within a week. As soon as the seeds have broken open and growth has begun the seeds can be planted.

Homemade Soap and Emergency Preparedness

Making soap is one of those old skills that used to be really common and now is nearly unheard of. If soap makers are ever again needed, learning it would give you a valuable skill that could help your family and community.

Soap Making Facts

Soap is actually a salt (source). It's the result of a chemical reaction between fat (an acid) and lye (sodium hydroxide [NaOH]) or potassium hydroxide (KOH) a base. Lye is also commercially sold as a plumbing solvent for clogged drains and is also used to preserve food.

Soap cannot be made without lye. It is possible to create a cleansing substance without lye, but it will not be soap. Sodium hydroxide is often used to make solid soap while potassium hydroxide is usually used to make softer soaps and liquid soap. For this article we will be using sodium hydroxide (NaOH) for a harder bar of soap.

The amount of lye needed to react with the fats and oils will vary depending on the chemical makeup of the fats and oils you are using. This is why it is important to use either established soap recipes or a lye calculator, when you make soap. A cup of olive oil may not need as much lye as the same amount of a different type of oil, so if you swap oils on the recipe you may end up with too much or too little lye. Too much lye means the soap will be caustic (capable of burning, corroding, or destroying living tissue); too little lye means the soap will contain too much fat, which will go rancid in time.

Cold-Processed Soap vs Hot-Processed Soap

Cold-processed soap still requires some heat, but not much. This soap making process requires exact measurements of lye and fat amounts and computing their ratio, using saponification charts or a lye calculator. With cold-processed soap, the bulk of the saponification happens after the combined oil and lye solution is poured into molds, usually over a period of two to six weeks. Because of this, cold-processed soap still contains glycerin which is generally considered good for human skin.

Hot-processed soaps are created by encouraging the saponification reaction by adding heat to speed up the reaction. Unlike cold-processed soap, in hot-processed soap, the oils are completely saponified by the end of the handling period. Therefore hot-processed soap is ready to use right away. In the "fully boiled hot-process" technique the glycerin and most of the impurities in the fat, lye, and water (which gives cold-pressed soap its color) are completely cooked out of the soap and drained off as a liquid to be repurposed, leaving a pure hard white bar.

Simple Cold Processed Soap

This recipe will make 25-30 nice bars of soap that will be kind to your skin that you could gift to friends and family. The lye is discounted at 7% (this means there is more fat in the recipe than the lye can convert to soap; the extra fat is good for your skin). You can make it as fancy or as simple as you want and it stores really well. I recommend that people learn how to make soap with this recipe, then move on to other recipes that may peak their interests.

First gather your equipment and pre-measured ingredients. Wear a long-sleeved shirt, rubber gloves, eye protection, keep your hair pulled back and wear shoes. Keep some vinegar nearby, so that if you get some lye on you (it will start to itch before it burns) you can treat it. Wash with plenty of soap and running water first and then rinse with vinegar. Same with surfaces; wash and rinse in case of spills then spray with vinegar and then repeat when you are finished making soap. If you get some on your clothes, immediately throw them in the washer.

32oz Cold Water

12oz Powdered Lye - pure sodium hydroxide (NaOH)

Add 32oz of water to the plastic container. In a well-ventilated area slowly add the lye into the water, stir gently trying not to splash. Never the other way around - you will get a violent volcano reaction. Always add lye to water. Set aside with one of the thermometers to cool to around 100° F - this could take several hours, to speed the process along set pitcher in an ice water bath or on a cold cement floor. If the lye has cooled too much vigorously stir the mixture, this will heat it back up.

In the large stainless steel or enamel stock pot add following solids, and then place over medium-low heat on the stove until all are liquefied:

> 24 oz Coconut Oil (coconut oil gives soap its bubbles and gives hardness to the bar, this is why most soap makers will tell you that bubbles to do not necessarily equal cleaning power).
>
> 28 oz White Shortening (Crisco will work)
>
> 10 oz Rendered Bacon Grease, or Rendered Tallow (click here to see How to Make Your Own Tallow) unsalted butter will also work. I don't do vegetarian soap, I live on a farmstead so I use animal fat in all my soaps.

Remove melted solids from heat (from here on out you are done with the stove, turn it off). Check your lye water temperature.

Add 24 oz of Olive Oil or vegetable oil

This will start lowering the fat temperature, you want it at 100° F as well (you can combine lye water and the oils anywhere between 125°F -100°F as long as they are the same temp or within 4 degrees of each other). Use the other cooking thermometer to check the temp. Once the temperature of the lye water and oils are the same, slowly stir the lye water into the melted fats and oils. Watch as the mixture begins to change color, get cloudy and thicken as the chemical reaction starts. You just made soap!

Stir the soap for 10 minutes, and then let it rest for 15 minutes, set a timer if you need reminding. Some people say to stir continuously, I have found this has no effect on how fast the soap finishes, so you might as well do something else for 15-20 minutes. Continue on this way until a thin layer of oil remains and the surface thickens to the point where you can see a trail where you just stirred (see picture below). This is called "trace," and it indicates that the soap is ready to be finished.

Hand stirred soap can take several hours to achieve "trace," to speed things along use a stick blender. Be sure to run the blender for a few minutes and then let it rest. Their cheap little motors will burn up if they are run continuously. Don't lift the bender above the liquid level, doing so will mix in a bunch of air into your soap. Trace can be achieved in as little as 5-10 minutes using a stick blender, but it can take longer.

Add 3 oz of any desired essential oils or any colorants and desired botanicals (like corn meal or oats for scrubbing power) an mix well at this point.

Finishing the Soap

Stir thoroughly, then pour into molds. If the mold does not have a lid, place a piece of butcher paper over top of the soap. This will help prevent soda ash from forming on the soap. Wrap with the towel, and place in an undisturbed dark area for 24 hours. Do not check on it. Leave it alone. After 24 hours remove the towel and let it sit for *another* 12 hours.

Cutting the Soap

After that point it should be a nice block of soap that you can pop out of the mold. Continue to wear gloves, at this point the soap is still caustic. Once out of the mold you may want to let it firm up for another day before cutting. A miter box can be used to cut straight bars. It's important to do this fairly early in the game, because if the soap firms up too much it will cut poorly and flake.

Collect the soap trimmings after cutting soap bars and press them together with your hands to make soap balls.

Set the bars somewhere dark to cure and harden uncovered for 2-6 weeks. Like wine, the longer cold pressed soap sits the better it will be. If you jump the gun and use your soap too soon it may burn you or it may just be too harsh, so it's important to let it sit.

Long Term Emergency Basic Soap Recipe

(recipe credit - Millersoap.com)

This recipe makes about 9 pounds of pure, hard, smooth no-nonsense soap suitable for hand washing, cleaning, laundry or soap flakes, follow this simple recipe:

> 13 oz. of lye
>
> 5 cups cold water
>
> 6 pounds clean fat (tallow or lard or some combination of both)

Follow the above procedures of making lye water, melting the fats, combining the two, stirring until trace, then adding to a mold. If you are in a cool area and it looks like the fat is starting to set up before the lye can convert it to soap (this is known as a false trace), apply some gentle heat to the bottom of the pot. A false trace may present itself as a really grainy texture. Stirring continuously and briskly for this recipe is better, when it starts to trace for real it will start to stick to the side of your pot.

There is nothing fancy about this recipe, the soap it produces will not lather real well, and may dry your skin - but it will get things clean. You may want to give this a try some day, and/or print the recipe out and keep it on hand just in case.

Log candle anyone?

It takes a lot of wood to build and maintain a bright, warm campfire. But what if there isn't much wood available, you want to stay warm and also be able to see in the dark? One possibility might be to make a log candle.

The idea is to make a controllable fire that provides warmth and light. The base doesn't heat up, so the fire won't melt down through the snow and put itself out. The log is prepared by cutting lengthways with a chainsaw for about 18 inches

Find a log about eight-to-12-inches in diameter.

Bury one end about knee-deep in the sand or dirt, so the log is securely anchored and immovable. In deep snow, it would probably be best to stomp down the snow, and then dig a hole for the log.

With a saw, cut lengthwise down from the top in pie-piece segments. The fire stops at the end of the cuts.

Load the cuts with pine pitch or other tinder or kindling and this is lit to ignite the log segments. Don't pack the cuts too tightly, or the air flow will be blocked.

How to plant a fruit tree

When to Plant

Fruit trees can be planted in early spring as soon as the frost in the ground has thawed. If your soil is waterlogged, wait until it drains to plant. You can also plant in the fall, but winter temperatures may damage young stock if you live in colder climates.

Bare-Root or Potted

Bare-root nursery stock is usually less expensive but it will still establish and grow well, if planted in April or early May. If you must store the trees a short time before planting, keep them in a cool, shady place where they will be out of the sun and wind. Pack the roots in moist sawdust or moss to prevent them from drying out. Potted or ball-and-burlap trees are preferable for planting dates in late May or early June, and are usually more expensive than bare root trees.

Choosing a Site

Pick a site with direct sunlight, preferable with southern exposer. It's also important to read the tag and do a little research to find out just how big your tree will get. Allow enough room for future growth between your tree and other buildings, avoid power lines and give other future trees space if you are planting more than one or want to plant additional trees in the future.

Site Prep

Set your tree in a bucket of water to soak while you dig the hole. Cut through the sod with a shovel and make a hole big enough for the root ball so the roots don't touch the edge of the hole anywhere. If you are planting your fruit trees in your lawn, set the chunks of sod aside so you can reapply them to the surface around the tree when you are done. Next, water the hole so the ground is nice and damp for the tree if your soil is on the dry side.

Pruning

Trim off any broken or dead sections of the tree's roots, also take this opportunity to prune your little tree, this may seem harsh as you haven't even planted it yet but it will often shock the tree into growing more aggressively, increasing it's chances of surviving the transplant.

Planting

When planting the tree, if you are concerned about poor soil, you can mix in some compost or peat moss at this time, but avoid fertilizer as it may damage the roots which are already in shock. If your tree has a 'graph union' (a point where they joined a branch to the rootstock – this will look like slight to sharp bend in the trunk, see above graphic) bury it so that the soil line is 2-3 inches below the union. If you have a dwarf or semi-dwarf trees and you bury the union, the tree will become a full sized tree. Position your tree in the hole so that one higher branch is facing south, this branch will give your tree shade during long hot days. Fill the hole with your soil of choice and compact it by gently stamping your feet around the base of the tree, reapply your sod if desired then water your tree with 2 full 5 gallon buckets of water pouring slowly so that it does not run off. Also consider staking or caging your new tree not only for support but also for protection against animals and for visibility.

Fertilizer and Water

After several weeks it should be okay to apply some fertilizer, although in some areas it is recommended you wait till the next growing season, check with your local county extension office for their advice on your area (click here for a general fact sheet on fertilizing fruit trees). Watering your new tree is also important to help get it started, especially in the first few weeks after planting. Try to apply five gallons of water around the base of the tree every week of the growing season in which there is less than an inch of rainfall.

Help making a fire

In an emergency, many media "experts" promote different ways to make sparks as a way to ignite a fire. But the advice sometimes fizzles out there. There may be a vague reference to catching the spark with some material called "tinder." Sometimes tree fungus or dry, rotted wood called "punk" is mentioned as a spark catcher. The media personality makes a spark somehow; there is a camera angle change, and presto! We have ignition! But in the real world, during an emergency, there isn't time to search for such specialized items, even if they are available, and even if they do work. Of all the fire making tools at your disposal, char cloth is one that should be included in every survival kit. It works with every method of fire making.

Char cloth is a material, usually 100 percent cotton that has been "cooked" like charcoal at high temperatures until it becomes black and flexible. Properly-made char cloth will easily catch a spark from any source and will spread into an ember. A spark can come from a flint and steel, flint stick, broken lighter, jumper cables and battery etc. You could even light char cloth with a damp match that flares but won't ignite. In fact, if you only have a few matches, (and matches are always a finite resource) your best move might be to light some char cloth. Once caught, a spark on char cloth is virtually impossible to blow out. If the tinder bundle and small kindling are ready, it should only take about a one-inch square of glowing char cloth to get a fire going. Lighted char cloth extinguishes easily with water. But all you have to do is dry the soaked material out and it will work again. Maybe the best thing about char cloth is that you make it yourself, and the materials are free. (Click how to make char cloth to learn how to make it!)

You could even make char cloth while you're lost if you took along a bandanna and an Altoids or similar tin. (It will give you something to do while sitting by your signal fire, waiting to be rescued!) You can also try charring some organic materials, such as tree bark (cedar and juniper) and others. Cattail fuzz works well, as does milkweed down in season. There might be a great natural charring material in your area, just waiting to be discovered. It goes without saying that any experimenting should first be done in your backyard!

Compost

What is Compost?

A mixture of various decaying organic substances, such as dead leaves, kitchen scraps, or manure, compost is used for fertilizing soil.

What Goes Into Compost?

Here's what you can include in your compost:

Kitchen scraps such as vegetable and fruit peelings, dried eggshells, tea bags, coffee grounds. If your fruits or veggies went bad before they were eaten, the compost bin is a perfect place for them.

Household items such as shredded newspapers and dryer lint can go into the compost bin, too.

Lawn clippings, leaves, dead plants, bark, wood chips, straw, and/or hay are important ingredients in your compost.

Manure from grass-eating (herbivore) animals, such as chickens, horses, and cows. (This is not necessary; however, if you can find a farmer or someone with horses that will let you haul away some manure, it will be wonderfully beneficial to your plants!)

Do not put these things into your compost:

- Bones, meat, wood ash, pet waste, fat, or dairy.
- Also, stay away from weeds – they might be ready to seed, in which case they could grow into new weeds.

What Do I Do With All of This Stuff?

- Set up a little bin or canister with a lid under your kitchen sink, or right next to it on the counter. Add your kitchen scraps to this until it is full. Take a second to chop anything big and/or really firm into smaller chunks, about 2-3 inch diameter, before adding it to your container.
- Set up your main compost pile outside. There are many options for setting up your compost pile, and what you choose depends on where you live, what kind of space you have, and how much you want to spend. Here's a quick run-down of the possibilities:

Make a pile directly on the ground, without a container. This works if you live in an area where don't have to worry about raccoons or neighbors who might be offended. It's free, and it's easy to turn the pile.

Build a compost bin. You can use old pallets, wood and wire, or wire mesh. This is relatively cheap and easy. The best size is about 3 x 3 x 3 feet.

Use a trash can and drill holes in the sides and top. This is also pretty cheap and very easy. It's a little more difficult to turn the pile this way, though, but it's possible; this has been our primary method.

Purchase a composting tumbler. These are pricey but oh, so lovely. You just put in your composting materials and turn the tumbler from time to time. Voila: compost.

Add your materials to the compost pile as you accumulate them, and make sure you turn it regularly, so the ingredients will mix together and oxygen will do its work in breaking them down.

Balancing the Contents of Your Compost

It's important to have a good balance of materials in your compost. Basically, you have two categories you need to consider:

> Greens (Nitrogen)
> Greens include grass, fruits, veggies, plants, manure, and other kitchen scraps.
> Browns (Carbon)
> Browns include leaves, bark, wood chips, and newspaper.

In general, you want to shoot for one part "green" to three parts "brown." Brown leaves are usually more abundant in autumn, while green grass clippings are more plentiful in spring and summer.

It may take a little time for you to find the proper balance for your compost pile. You can ask neighbors to save grass clippings and leaves, and your city may have a facility where large brush is converted into wood chips; get creative about resources! However, plenty of people are able to make their own compost without needing to go to any of these extra lengths.

In the end, your compost will be ready to use when it is a dark, rich, slightly moist soil-like substance, having no bad odor, but instead smelling like you would imagine the scent of a forest floor.

Compost your livestock manure. Manure is a very valuable and underutilized resource. It's estimated that one horse can produce $175 a year or more in compost, with cattle doing a little better than that. Start by using a cart attached to a tractor or ATV or you can even use a wheelbarrow. Survey your property a few times each month, and pick up all the manure.

Combine that manure with any used shavings, straw, or grass clippings you may have and form a compost pile. You can make a large bin with treated lumber to hold the manure, if you aren't concerned about how a compost pile will look on your property or you can simply make a pile - making sure it's located on flat ground to reduce run off .

Heat: Although the composting process will occur naturally over several months or years, with human help the entire process can be completed in as little as 4-6 weeks. Four essential ingredients are needed: oxygen, moisture, and a proper Carbon:Nitrogen ratio. When these components are present, the compost will heat up naturally to approximately 130-140º F. This heat will kill most internal parasites and many weed seeds present in the manure. If you are composting correctly, you won't be breeding flies.

Oxygen: The decomposition process takes place when particle surfaces come in contact with air. To increase oxygen intake, turn your compost piles / bins as often as possible (anywhere from 3 times per week to a few times per month). The more you turn, the faster you reach the end result. Turning the pile can be done by hand or with a tractor. Increase the surface area by chopping, shredding, or breaking up the material speeds up the composting process. If the compost lacks oxygen, it will have a bad odor.

Moisture: Your compost pile should be about the consistency of a well wrung-out sponge. You don't want it too wet and you don't want it too dry. If the compost appears too wet, turn it or add dry materials such as leaves or straw. If it's too dry, simply add some water. Maintain moisture levels by covering your compost piles with either composting fabric or plastic tarps.

Carbon:Nitrogen: Carbon and nitrogen are the two fundamental elements in composting. The bacteria and fungi that break down the manure and turn it into compost are fueled by carbon and nitrogen. The bulk of your compost pile should be carbon with just enough nitrogen thrown in to aid in the decomposition process. Carbon is found in 'browns' (leaves, sawdust, straw, shredded newspaper, ashes, cornstalks) and higher nitrogen is available in 'greens' (clover, manures, alfalfa, garden waste, grass clippings, hay, seaweed, weeds). If you have too much nitrogen, ammonia gas will be produced and you'll notice a foul odor. The ideal C:N ratio is 25-30:1. Below are some examples of materials that might be added to your compost and their corresponding C:N ratios.

Source Carbon:Nitrogen ratio

Manure 15:1
Dry Weeds 90:1
Weeds (fresh) 25:1
Cardboard 300-400:1
Grass clippings 15-20:1
Pine Needles 80:1
Alfalfa 12:1
Seaweed 20:1
Vegetable waste/produce 19-25:1
Garden Waste 30:1?
Leaves 50-60:1
Sawdust 300-400:1 ?

Wood chips 500-600:1 ?

Straw, cornstalks 60-80:1

Locate your pile in a spot that tends to remain dry so that you can access the pile with equipment to turn it when needed. To reach the proper temperatures, a compost pile needs to be at least 3 feet square by 3-4 feet high. Composting in a bin decreases the size required for adequate temperatures, but involves more cost initially.

Compost piles are combustible. Keep your pile away from housing facilities, and just like hay storage facilities, don't allow smoking near your compost piles! If a pile smells like alcohol, the conditions are ripe for combustion. DO NOT add water at this time; instead, turn the pile to aerate it. Your compost pile will cool off on its own and will be approximately 1/2 its original size. Finished compost will smell and look like rich soil!

You can take this compost and use it on your own garden and save money not having to buy fertilizer, or you can sell it to your neighbors, or spread it on your pasture. Livestock grazing on pastures spread with composted manure (instead of fresh manure) are more likely to graze normally and are less likely to restrict grazing to areas with the thinnest application rates. Your pasture will produce more grass meaning you will have to buy less hay.

Handy Tip: To find buyers for your composted manure contact local topsoil companies, tree farms, landscapers, and organic farmers. A sign out on the road will also help. There's a good chance that you will need to deliver it to them but selling your extra compost can allow you to use that money for your critters - this allows them to pay for their keep even more than just providing eggs, milk or meat.

Making rustic country bread

Sponge

1/2 tsp active dry yeast (not rapid rise)

1 cup water 1 cup bread flour

1 cup whole wheat Dough;

3 1/2 cups bread flour

1/2 cup rye flour

1 1/2 cups water (room temp)

2 tbs honey

2 tsp salt coarse cornmeal to sprinkle on peel{A flat, smooth, shovel like tool used to slide pizzas and yeast breads onto a BAKING STONE or BAKING SHEET in an oven.} Sponge; Sit out your 1 cup of water and allow it to reach room temp. Takes about 20

minutes.

Once your water comes to room temperature, mix the yeast with water in a bowl until dissolved, add the two flours and use a rubber spatula to pull the water through the flour and mix the two flours. You will end up with this. This would be your sponge. Cover and set aside. We will come back to it in 5 hours or overnight. Our sponge has sat for 5 hours now.

On top of this you will want to add all but 2 cups of the bread flour, and all the remaining ingredients.

Use a wooden spoon to mix and build up the gluten, 5 minutes.

Work in the remaining flour before turning out onto a floured surface.

Dough will be sticky, but here is where most people make their mistakes, do not add any more then 1/4 cup of extra flour, and do not knead bread longer than required.

As I said it will be sticky, just pat your hands in the 1/4 cup flour as needed. The dough will become silky after a few minutes.

Knead your bread for a total of 5 minutes, before placing into a lightly greased bowl, cover and allow to triple in size, 2 hours.

Two hours have passed, and your dough should be tripled in size. Turn it out onto a floured surface, and round it.

Flour a cheesecloth or linen and line a colander.

Place rounded dough in, cover with foil and allow to double in size, 45 minutes.

In the meantime, place an empty pan onto the lower rack of your oven, and preheat the oven to 450F.

After you have allowed the dough to double in size sprinkle your peel with corn meal. If you do not have a stone or brick oven, you will not need to do this. But you do need a baking stone, sprinkle the corn meal directly onto this.

Invert the colander over the stone and gently set the dough down. Carefully remove the linen or cheesecloth.

Pour 2 cups water into the preheated pot we placed in earlier.

Place 3 slits onto the top of the dough, and slide into the oven. Bake for 25 minutes, turn and bake for another 10 minutes.

Turn off oven and open the door, allow bread to sit in the oven for another 10 minutes

Remove from oven and allow to cool 2 hours before cutting

Making a fire with Vaseline

Materials to use:

Petroleum Jelly

Toilet Paper roll

Cotton Balls or Dryer Lint

Lighter

Toilet paper rolls, petroleum jelly, dryer lint, applicator stick

Rather than using cotton balls, I prefer to use dryer lint and toilet paper rolls as it keeps the waste down by re-purposing them.

Step one:

Use a stick, a spoon or a knife to spread the petroleum jelly on the cotton balls or dryer lint. Be very careful not to get this stuff on your fingers, clothes or any other flammable materials. When ignited it's like napalm.

I demonstrated with the following photo in case you don't happen to have a toilet paper roll. It's actually easier (and cleaner) to just use your stick to wipe off the petroleum jelly inside the roll first, and then stuff the cotton or dryer lint into the roll.

Spreading petroleum jelly on dryer lint (That is a concrete floor by the way, DO NOT do this on carpet or a flammable surface.)

Step two:

Stuff the dryer lint into the toilet paper roll, and place the roll into your fireplace or fire pit underneath your wood.

Step three:

Thoroughly wipe off any petroleum jelly that you may have gotten on yourself.

Step four:

Ignite the toilet paper roll and lint. I prefer to use a long utility lighter that keeps my hand away from the fire.

And there you have it. No paper or even kindling needed.

Homemade deodorant

Ingredients:

5-6 Tbsp Coconut oil

1/4 cup baking soda

1/4 cup arrowroot powder or cornstarch

Combine equal portions of baking soda & arrowroot powder.

Then slowly add coconut oil and work it in with a spoon until it maintains the substance you desire. It should be about the same texture as the store bought kind, solid but able to be applied easily.

You can either scoop this into your old dispensers or place in a small container with lid and apply with fingers with each use.

After applying the product, you can just rub the remains into your hands as a lotion!

This recipe lasts about 3 months for two people with regular daily use.

Here are my notes from my experience:

I suggest corn starch instead of arrowroot powder (much cheaper).

It doesn't explain that coconut oil is hard at room temperature, so I put the jar in a pot of shallow water and heated it on the stove for a bit to soften it.

The coconut smell goes away once it's cooled down; don't worry you won't smell like suntan lotion when you wear it!

I ended up putting in way more corn starch and baking soda (equal parts) than it called for because it wasn't solidifying like it said it would -- turns out I think the oil was just too warm, but no harm done. If it seems like you've put in too much, put the jar in the fridge for a bit to see if it thickens up a bit.

Keep in mind unless you somehow pour it into an old deodorant container, you'll be scooping it out with your fingers to apply it (mine's in a small mason jar.) It seems weird at first, but if you take a shower every day it's not a big deal, you're just touching your own skin! Like the blog says, you can rub the extra stuff into your hands and use it as lotion because coconut oil is great for skin.

On really hot days, it'll separate a bit, but you can just stir it up.

I think the coconut oil is the most expensive part, but it lasts long enough to still be a bargain compared to buying regular stuff. The jar I'm finishing up now was made in January, so I've gotten at least 7 months out of less than $10!

Also -- this is of course *not* an antiperspirant. It's unnatural to block your pores from sweating, so I don't use those, this is deodorant only. But it works! I rode my bike 6 mi. one day last month when it was in the 80's-90's and it held up wonderfully. I've been meaning to compile my notes into my own blog entry, but until I have the time to do so I'll have to settle for this. Sorry it's a bit of a mess.

Building an Ozone Generator

Transformer with its power ranging from 3000 v to 7500 v. (the best place to look for one is at the neon sign dealer.)

2 glass jars (one small, one large. The small jar should fit well in the large jar. Glass from photo frames can also be used.)

Copper, brass, aluminum scrap foil or used razor blades

Wooden board, to mount the transformer

Wires or cords

Plug

Glue gun of high temperature

Alligator clips

How to Build an Ozone Generator at Home

Step 1

Put the copper, brass or aluminum scrap that you have in the small glass jar. Care should be taken, that the base of the jar is completely covered with the foil. Similarly, foil the large jar as well. When you are using foil, then fold the foil multiple times and then place it, at the bottom of the jar.

Step 2

Place the small jar inside the big jar. Stick the two jars with glue. In case you do not have glue gun; be careful when you choose the jars, the small jar should fit into the large jar snugly. The large jar is used as an insulating agent.

Step 3

Place the jars on the wooden board. The transformer should also be placed next to the jars on the wooden board itself. The alligator clips should be attached to both end of the wires. Now plug the alligator clips to the end of the transformer lead. This should be followed by attaching the next clip to the aluminum foil inside the larger jar and the other clip should be attached to the foil in the smaller jar. In other words, one end of both the wires should be attached to the transformer, while the other ends should be inside large and small jar respectively. Care should be taken to ensure that the two wires that connect inside the larger and the smaller jar, do not come in contact with each other, as they may spark.

Step 4

Fasten the set up on the wooden board, so that the entire device is well insulated. If a wooden board is not available, any other insulator can also be used. The transformer can now be plugged in safely.

There are certain indicators, which can be of help, to know whether the homemade ozone generator is working as expected. The indicators are:

When you plug the generator, there is a possibility of crackling noise from the generator. If there is indeed a crackling noise, then it means that the device is working properly.

If the generator is placed in a dark room, a purple or a blue emission is seen from the jar. Then the ozone can be smelled immediately.

In case a yellow glow is emitted, it's an indicator that the glass is broken. In that case you will have to replace the glass jar. For doing so unplug the transformer first and then replace the glass jar.

Ozone can also be used as a deodorizer. It is beneficial to humans, animals and plants alike. It can be used to kill bacteria in the house. But overexposure to ozone can be dangerous. Therefore, care should be taken to ensure one does not leave the ozone generator on, when one is hitting the sack. The ozone generator should not be used in humid areas, as its reaction with metals leads, in these areas, can lead to metal corrosion

Building a windmill to charge batteries

Things You'll Need
    Measuring tape
    Alternator (with disk attached)
    1/4 inch nuts, bolts and washers
    Drill with 1/4 carbide drill bit
    5 inch diameter, 25 inch length of PVC pipe
    Skill saw
    600 grit sand paper
    Plastic pop bottle
    1 foot by 6 inch length of cutting board (plastic)
    Hot glue gun (with glue)
    Zip tie
    (Optional) diverter, rectifier, ceramic heating element and water heater

Instructions

1. Obtain an alternator of the type that is used in older vehicles (without electronics built into it). Make sure it is the kind of alternator that has the metal disk/face attached to the front of it. This is where the blades will be bolted down. The

alternator can be bought 'used' but if it is bought new it will last longer. Buy 1/4 inch bolts, nuts and washers that fit with them. Also buy a section of PVC pipe that is 25 inches long and 5 inches in diameter.

2. Look at the plate that comes on the end of the alternator. There will be four screw holes on it. Drill them out so that the 1/4 inch bolts fit through them. Drill holes halfway between these holes and the central axle, making sure not to get so close to the axle that the bolts will get in the way of the pivoting face of the alternator.

3. Cut the pipe in half the long way down (on opposite sides of the pipe) while making sure the cut edge is as straight as possible. Take half of the pipe and measure 1/4 of the way from one edge at one end and 1/4 of the way from the opposite edge at the other end of the pipe. Use a piece of tape to make a diagonal line from one of these measurements to the other. Then use a skill saw to cut as straight a line as possible from one mark to the other mark near the opposite corner.

4. Drill bolt holes that will fit the blades onto the alternator at the wide end of the pipe cuttings. The blade should be positioned radial to the central axle. Do any further trimming on the edges of the blades using a joiner or plane if desired to reduce vibration. Sharpen the leading edge (the straight edge of the blades) by sanding with 600 grit sand paper. The blades are already contoured from the natural curve in the pipe.

5. Bolt the blade on by inserting the bolts from the back to the front so that the bolts stick out the front and don't catch on anything. Make sure that there are washers on either side of the bolts as they pierce the holes in the blades that were made earlier. Tighten the nuts on the bolts by hand, being careful not to crack the PVC blades.

6. Use plastic from a pop bottle and zip ties to cover the housing so that the alternator is protected from water. First cut the plastic sheets from the water bottle and then use zip ties to secure the plastic around the alternator.

7. Cut a 1 foot by 6 inch length of cutting board. Hold the board the long way and trace the pattern that you will cut. At one end, draw a line 2 inches (1/3 of the way) from one of the edges and draw this line for 6 inches. At this point, let the line taper out to the far edge at a rate of 2 inches to the side per inch forward. When you are done, the board should look like half of a paddle with the dividing line straight down the middle. Attach the "handle" of the paddle with the dividing line against the housing of the generator with some hot glue and then zip tie the handle onto the generator.

You can also use the alternator method with vertical axis windmills. Make sure that if you are using a generator to charge batteries, you use a rectifier (to keep the batteries from turning the alternator like a motor). Use a diverter to siphon off electricity once the battery is charged to prevent overcharging the batteries and ruining them. Some people have the diverter go to a ceramic heating element that they use to heat water in a water heater.

This generator should be fine for medium wind locations but if the wind gets too furious, a braking mechanism should be applied or the generator should be temporarily taken out of service. If the generator is left up, there is a chance that the wind can get fast enough to tear the blades apart and throw them outwards as dangerous projectiles. Please see the resources for an example of this problem on a professional-sized wind generator.

Make a welder with two car batteries

1. Hook two car batteries together
2. Take jumper cables out
3. Hook positive side to the metal you are welding
4. Hook negative side to a wrench clamped down on a stick of solder
5. Don't look at the spark (takes time to heat up)

Inedible and Edible plants

Plants to Avoid

If you can't clearly identify a plant and you don't know if it's poisonous, it's better to be safe than sorry. Steer clear from a plant if it has:

Milky or discolored sap
Spines, fine hairs, or thorns
Beans, bulbs, or seeds inside pods
Bitter or soapy taste
Dill, carrot, parsnip, or parsley-like foliage
"Almond" scent in the woody parts and leaves
Grain heads with pink, purplish, or black spurs
Three-leaved growth pattern

Many toxic plants will exhibit one or more of the above characteristics. Bear in mind that some of the plants we suggest below have some of these attributes, yet they're still edible. The characteristics listed are just guidelines for when you're not confident about what you're dealing with. If you want to be completely sure that an unknown plant is edible, and you have a day or two to spare, you can always perform the Universal Edibility Test.

Amaranth (Amaranthus retroflexus and other species)

Native to the Americas but found on most continents, amaranth is an edible weed. You can eat all parts of the plant, but be on the lookout for spines that appear on some of the leaves. While not poisonous, amaranth leaves do contain oxalic acid and may contain large amounts of nitrates if grown in nitrate-rich soil. It's recommended that you boil the leaves to remove the oxalic acid and nitrates. Don't drink the water after you boil the plant. With that said, you can eat the plant raw if worse comes to worst.

Asparagus (Asparagus officinalis)

The vegetable that makes your pee smell funny grows in the wild in most of Europe and parts of North Africa, West Asia, and North America. Wild asparagus has a much thinner stalk than the grocery-store variety. It's a great source of source of vitamin C, thiamine, potassium and vitamin B6. Eat it raw or boil it like you would your asparagus at home.

Burdock (Arctium lappa)

Medium to large-sized plant with big leaves and purplish thistle-like flower heads. The plant is native to the temperate areas of the Eastern Hemisphere; however, it has been naturalized in parts of the Western Hemisphere as well. Burdock is actually a popular food in Japan. You can eat the leaves and the peeled stalks of the plant either raw or boiled. The leaves have a bitter taste, so boiling them twice before eating is recommended to remove the bitterness. The root of the plant can also be peeled, boiled, and eaten.

Cattail (Typha)

Known as cattails or punks in North America and bullrush and reedmace in England, the typha genus of plants is usually found near the edges of freshwater wetlands. Cattails were a staple in the diet of many Native American tribes. Most of a cattail is edible. You can boil or eat raw the rootstock, or rhizomes, of the plant. The rootstock is usually found underground. Make sure to wash off all the mud. The best part of the stem is near the bottom where the plant is mainly white. Either boil or eat the stem raw. Boil the leaves like you would spinach. The corn dog-looking female flower spike can be broken off and eaten like corn on the cob in the early summer when the plant is first developing. It actually has a corn-like taste to it.

Clovers (Trifolium)

Lucky you - clovers are actually edible. And they're found just about everywhere there's an open grassy area. You can spot them by their distinctive trefoil leaflets. You can eat clovers raw, but they taste better boiled.

Chicory (Cichorium intybus)

You'll find chicory growing in Europe, North America, and Australia. It's a bushy plant with small blue, lavender, and white flowers. You can eat the entire plant. Pluck off the young leaves and eat them raw or boil them. The chicory's roots will become tasty after boiling. And you can pop the flowers in your mouth for a quick snack. You can also dry the Chicory root, grind it up and make a sort of coffee substitute from it.

Chickweed (Stellaria media)

You'll find this herb in temperate and arctic zones. The leaves are pretty hefty, and you'll often find small white flowers on the plant. They usually appear between May and July. You can eat the leaves raw or boiled. They're high in vitamins and minerals.

Curled Dock (Rumex crispus)

You can find curled dock in Europe, North America, South America, and Australia. It's distinguished by a long, bright red stalk that can reach heights of three feet. You can eat the stalk raw or boiled. Just peel off the outer layers first. It's recommend that you boil the leaves with several changes of water in order to remove its naturally bitter taste.

Dandelion (Taraxacum officinale)

Sure, it's an obnoxious weed on your perfectly mowed lawn, but when you're out in the wild this little plant can save your life. The entire plant is edible- roots, leaves, and flower. Eat the leaves while they're still young; mature leaves taste bitter. If you do decide to eat the mature leaves, boil them first to remove their bitter taste. Boil the roots before eating as well. You can drink the water you boiled the roots in as a tea and use the flower as a garnish for your dandelion salad.

Field Pennycress (Thalspi vulgaris)

Field Pennycress is a weed found in most parts of the world. Its growing season is early spring to late winter. You can eat the seeds and leaves of field pennycress raw or boiled. The only caveat with field pennycress is not to eat it if it's growing in contaminated soil. Pennycress is a hyperaccumulator of minerals, meaning it sucks up any and all minerals around it. General rule is don't eat pennycress if it's growing by the side of the road or is near a Superfund site.

Fireweed (Epilobium angustifolium)

This pretty little plant is found primarily in the Northern Hemisphere. You can identify fireweed by its purple flower and the unique structure of the leaves' veins; the veins are circular rather than terminating on the edges of the leaves. Several Native American tribes included fireweed in their diet. It's best eaten young when the leaves are tender. Mature fireweed plants have tough and bitter tasting leaves. You can eat the stalk of the plant as well. The flowers and seeds have a peppery taste. Fireweed is a great source of vitamins A and C.

Green Seaweed (Ulva lactuca)

If you're ever shipwrecked on a deserted island, fish the waters near the beach for some green seaweed. This stuff is found in oceans all over the world. After you pull green seaweed from the water, rinse with fresh water if available and let it dry. You can eat it raw or include it in a soup. Or if you're particularly enterprising, catch a fish with your homemade spear and use the seaweed to make sushi rolls, sans rice.

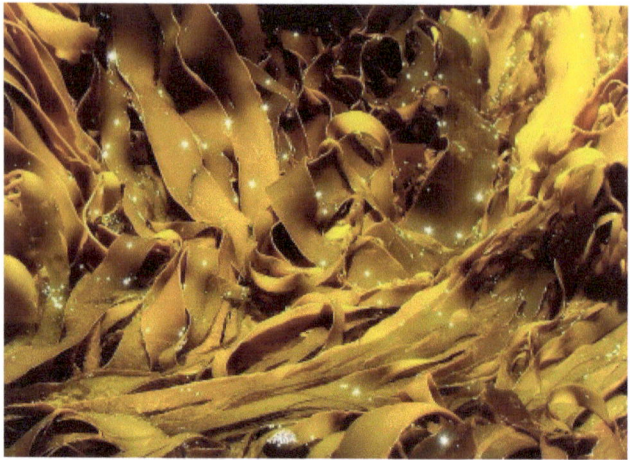

Kelp (Alaria esculenta)

Kelp is another form of seaweed. You can find it in most parts of the world. Eat it raw or include it in a soup. Kelp is a great source of folate, vitamin K, and lignans.

Plantain (Plantago)

Found in all parts of the world, the plantain plant (not to be confused with the banana-like plantain) has been used for millennia by humans as a food and herbal remedy for all sorts of maladies. You can usually find plantains in wet areas like marshes and bogs, but they'll also sprout up in alpine areas. The oval, ribbed, short-stemmed leaves tend to hug the ground. The leaves may grow up to about 6? long and 4? wide. It's best to eat the leaves when they're young. Like most plants, the leaves tend to get bitter tasting as they mature. Plantain is very high in vitamin A and calcium. It also provides a bit of vitamin C.

Prickly Pear Cactus (Opuntia)

Found in the deserts of North America, the prickly pear cactus is a very tasty and nutritional plant that can help you survive the next time you're stranded in the desert. The fruit of the prickly pear cactus looks like a red or purplish pear. Hence the name. Before eating the plant, carefully remove the small spines on the outer skin or else it will feel like you're swallowing a porcupine. You can also eat the young stem of the prickly pear cactus. It's best to boil the stems before eating.

Purslane (Portulaca oleracea)

While considered an obnoxious weed in the United States, purslane can provide much needed vitamins and minerals in a wilderness survival situation. Ghandi actually numbered purslane among his favorite foods. It's a small plant with smooth fat leaves that have a refreshingly sour taste. Purslane grows from the beginning of summer to the start of fall. You can eat purslane raw or boiled. If you'd like to remove the sour taste, boil the leaves before eating.

Sheep Sorrel (Rumex acetosella)

Sheep sorrel is native to Europe and Asia but has been naturalized in North America. It's a common weed in fields, grasslands, and woodlands. It flourishes in highly acidic soil. Sheep sorrel has a tall, reddish stem and can reach heights of 18 inches. Sheep sorrel contains oxalates and shouldn't be eaten in large quantities. You can eat the leaves raw. They have a nice tart, almost lemony flavor.

White Mustard (Synapsis alba)

White mustard is found in the wild in many parts of the world. It blooms between February and March. You can eat all parts of the plant- seeds, flowers, and leaves.

Wood Sorrel (Oxalis)

You'll find wood sorrel in all parts of the world; species diversity is particularly rich in South America. Humans have used wood sorrel for food and medicine for millennia. The

Kiowa Indians chewed on wood sorrel to alleviate thirst, and the Cherokee ate the plant to cure mouth sores. The leaves are a great source of vitamin C. The roots of the wood sorrel can be boiled. They're starchy and taste a bit like a potato.

Plants of Medical use

Marijuana

Seriously. Though marijuana is still illegal in most of the United States, it is legal in 12 states for medicinal purposes, and if a case of poison ivy in the woods isn't a medicinal purpose, what is? Marijuana was "mostly" legal until 1970 when it became classified as a hard drug. No one thought of it as a dangerous or illicit drug until the 20th century; in fact, hemp was George Washington's primary crop and Thomas Jefferson's secondary crop. The Declaration of Independence is written on it; the Gutenberg Bible was printed on hemp, too. There's actually an environmental dimension to legalizing marijuana – hemp is a remarkable and renewable plant, offering all kinds of foodstuff and product uses that surpass cotton and plastic. But health benefits are well documented, from depression and anxiety relief to reduced blood pressure, pain alleviation and glaucoma treatment. It is not addictive, does not kill brain cells and is not a "gateway" drug – in fact, when pot is more available, studies show that the use of hard drugs like heroin and cocaine actually decreases. The bottom line for hikers: when your leg is broken from a misjudged boulder hopping attempt (pain) and a bear has eaten your friend (depression) and you're lost because you forgot the compass (dumbass), consult the cannabis.

Yarrow

Achilleus, the greatest hero of the Trojan War in Homer's "Iliad", is reported to have used yarrow to stop the flow of blood from his wounds inflicted in battle. It has been scientifically proven that this plant has substances that have blood clotting and anti-inflammatory properties. In the Middle Ages in Europe, yarrow tea was taken to stop internal bleeding. Micmac Indians drank it with warm milk to treat upper respiratory infections.

Alcea rosea, Hollyhock

The flowers are used in the treatment of respiratory and inflammatory ailments and the root extracts to produce marshmallow sweets.

Alchemilla vulgaris, Lady's Mantle

The common English name is accounted for by the leaves resemblance to a cloak worn by English women in medieval times. A preparation of dried leave was used to control diarrhea and to stop bleeding.

Allium cepa, Onion

Like garlic, onions contain antibiotics and substances that lower blood sugar, serum cholesterol and blood pressure. Onion juice sweetened with sugar or honey is a traditional remedy for colds and coughs. Onions are rich in vitamins B-1, B-2 and Vitamin C.

Allium sativum, Garlic

It has been used for centuries for medicinal purposes and as a culinary herb. In the Talmud Book of Ezra, Jews are encouraged to partake of garlic at the Friday night Shabbat meal for the following five reasons: (1) to keep the body warm; (2) to brighten the face; (3) to kill intestinal parasites; (4) to increase the volume of semen; and (5) to foster love and to do away with jealousy. Garlic is mentioned more than twenty times in the ancient Egyptian medical papyrus called the Codex Ebers dating back to ca. 1550 B.C. Pliny the Elder sited more than sixty therapeutic uses for garlic. Dioscorides, chief physician for the Roman army, prescribed garlic for intestinal parasitic disorders.

Garlic oil was first isolated in 1844. More than one hundred compounds have been identified as constituents of garlic oil. In the Middle Ages, it was eaten daily as a protection against the bubonic plagues that ravished the European continent. Louis Pasteur described its antibacterial properties in 1858. Tons of garlic were used in World War I in field dressings to prevent infection. Alliin and allicin are sulfur-containing compounds that are antibacterial and anti-fungal. When garlic cloves are sliced, diced, or minced, alliin converts allicin into a large number of thioallyl compounds that are effective in lowering blood pressure, blood sugar, serum cholesterol and serum triglycerides It is effective in boosting the immune system. Garlic is a natural pesticide against mosquito larvae.

Allium schoenoprasum, Chives

In traditional folk medicine Chives were eaten to treat and purge intestinal parasites, enhance the immune system, stimulate digestion, and treat anemia.

Garlic and scallions, along with onions, leeks, chives, and shallots, are rich in flavonols, substances in plants that have been shown to have anti-tumor effects. New research from China confirms that eating vegetables from the allium group (allium is Latin for garlic) can reduce the risk of prostate cancer.

Allium tuberosum, Garlic Chives

In Chinese herbal medicine, garlic chives have been used to treat fatigue, control excessive bleeding, and as an antidote for ingested poisons. The leaves and bulbs are applied to insect bites, cuts, and wounds, while the seeds are used to treat kidney, liver, and digestive system problems.

Althea officinalis, True Marshmallow

It is a native of Asia that has been naturalized in America. Marshmallow syrup from the roots is used in treating coughs and irritated throats.

Anchusa officinalis, Bugloss

Preparations made from roots and/or stems have been used in modern folk medicine primarily as an expectorant (to raise phlegm) or as an emollient (a salve to sooth and soften the skin).

Anethum graveolens 'Fernleaf', Dill

Dill is recorded as a medicinal plant for at least five thousand years in the writings of the Egyptians. Oil extracted from the seeds is made into potions and given to colicky babies. Adults take the preparation to relieve indigestion.

Angelica archangelica, Angelica

Though all parts of the plant are medicinal, preparations are made mainly from the roots. Its medicinal uses include: relief of ingestion, flatulence and colic; improvements of peripheral arterial circulation e.g. Buerger's disease; a tonic for bronchitis

Anthemis nobilis a.k.a Chamaemelum nobile, Roman Chamomile

It is used for the relief of gastric distress. Peter Rabbit's mother treated Peter with chamomile tea to alleviate the distress that followed the overindulgence of eating too much in Mr. McGregor's vegetable garden. Roman Chamomile resembles German Chamomile. Both Chamomiles are members of the same family. They have pale green feathery leaves and have flowers that resemble daisies with an apple-like fragrance.

Antirrhinum majus, Snapdragon

Preparations made from leaves and flowers are used to reduce fever and inflammation. In a poultice, it can be applied to the body surface to treat burns, infections and hemorrhoids.

Apium graveolens, Celery

Essential oils have a sedative and anticonvulsant effect, and are used in the treatment of hypertension. Seeds used to treat arthritis and urinary tract infections.

Aquilegia Canadensis, Columbine

Preparations of this plant are used as an astringent, analgesic, and a diuretic. American Indians used crushed seeds to relieve headaches.

Artemisia vulgaris, Mugwort

It is a natural insect repellant of moths as well as a culinary herb used in flavoring foods such as poultry stuffing. It is alleged to have many medicinal properties from hastening and easing labor to producing sedation. Its medicinal properties are questionable.

Asarum Euopeaum, European Ginger

In the past, it was used as an emetic, but it is obsolete because of toxicity. It is similar in use to Asarum canadense which was used by American Indians in the form of a root tea to treat respiratory, cardiac and "female" ailments. Asarum canadense contains aristocholic acid, an anti-tumor compound.

Asclepius Incarnata, Butterfly Weed

It is used primarily in the treatment of respiratory disorders. Its uses are very similar to those of Asclepias tuberosa.

Asclepias tuberosa, Butterfly Weed or Pleurisy Root

This plant is native to North America. Omaha Indians ate the raw root to treat bronchitis and taught the pioneers to do the same. It is an expectorant; it promotes coughing that raises phlegm. It also contains cardiac glycosides and an estrogen-like substance. It is a component of Lydia E. Pinkham's Vegetable Compound (1875 to 1960) advertised for use in "womb trouble, sick headache, and nervous breakdowns".

Asperula odorata, Sweet Woodruff

Research suggests that it may have anti-arthritic properties. Historically, it has been used to treat liver disorders. In Germany, it is an essential ingredient in May wine drunk as a "spring tonic". The fragrance of dry leaves gives linen closets a sweet aroma that keeps moths away.

Baptisia Australis, Blue False Indigo

American Indians used root tea as an emetic (to produce vomiting) and as a laxative. Root poultices were used to reduce inflammation, and held in the mouth against an aching tooth.

Food Charts

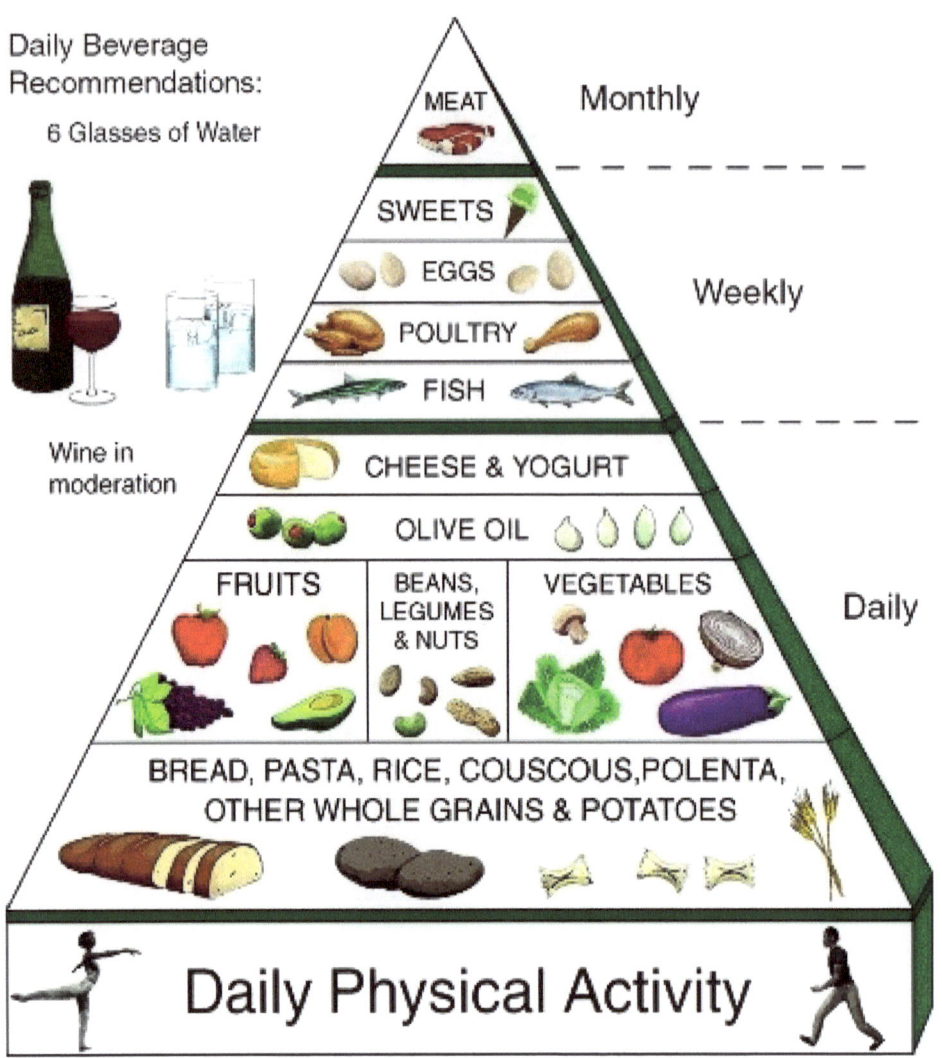

FOOD CONTENT CHART

Food	Grams Protein	Grams Carbohydrates	Grams Fat	Grams Fiber	Calories
BREADS					
1 slice white bread	2	12	1	<1	65
1 slice whole wheat bread	2	12	1	2	65
1 hamburger bun	3	20	2	<1	115
½ plain bagel	3	18	1	1	90
1 biscuit	2	14	3	<1	94
1 small muffin	3	20	5	<1	135
1 serving combread	3	15	4	2	100
BREAKFAST CEREALS					
¾ cup raisin bran	3	30	1	4	130
¾ cup cornflakes	2	24	0	.1	110
¾ cup Cheerios	3	16	1	2	90
¾ cup Captain Crunch	2	30	3	1	156
¾ cup Golden Grahams	2	33	2	2	156
½ cup Nature Valley Granola	12	76	20	12	503
¾ cup oatmeal, cooked	5	26	3	4	150
MISCELLANEOUS GRAINS					
1 4-inch pancake	2	9	2	1	60
1 waffle	7	27	8	1	205
½ cup cooked spaghetti, plain	3	20	1	<1	110
½ cup white rice, cooked	2	28	0	1	132
½ cup brown rice, cooked	3	22	2	4	110
½ cup whole wheat noodles	4	20	1	4	130

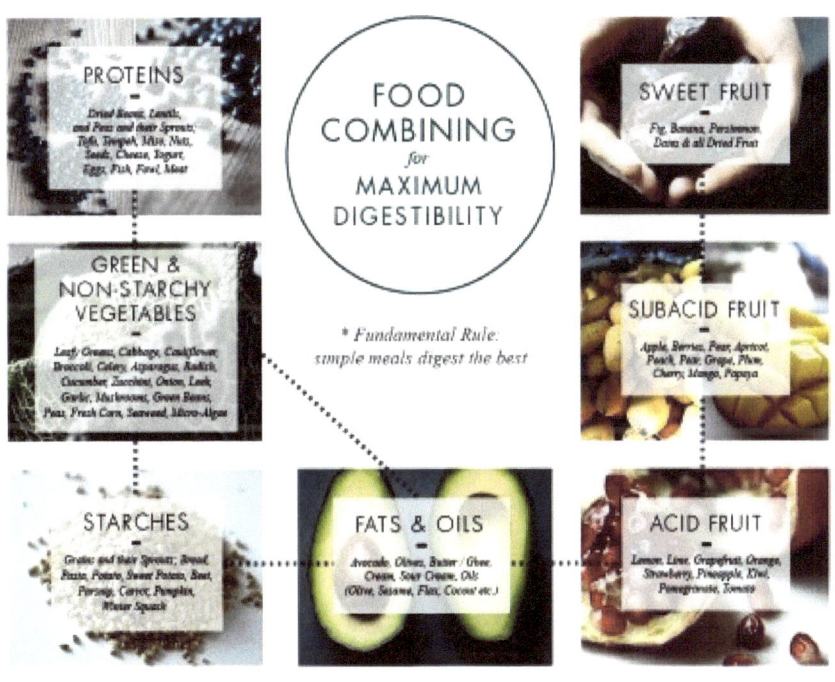

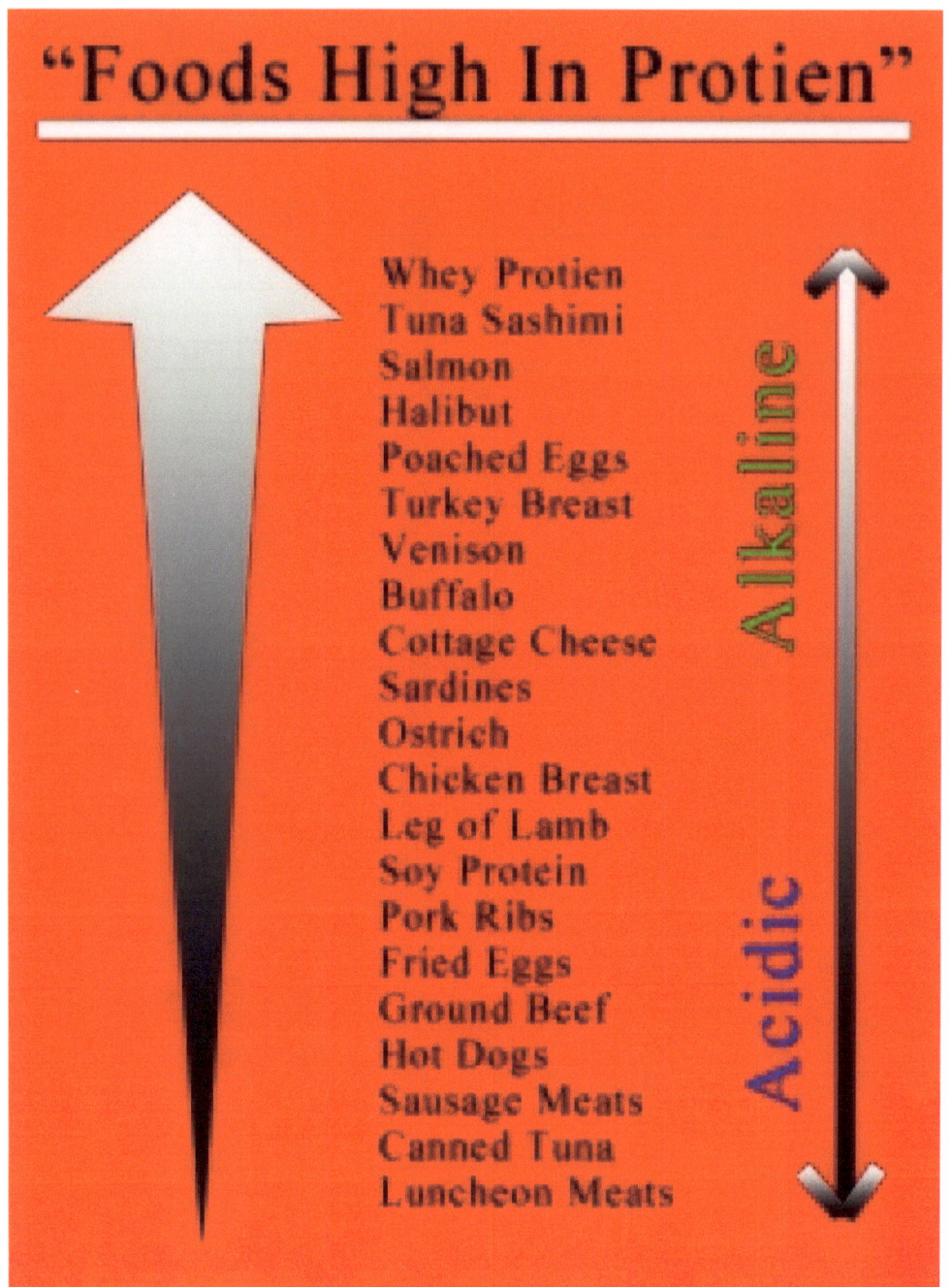

"Food suggestions after a physically exhausting day"

Cardio Day:
Oatmeal w/milk & banana

Toast w/ cottage

Cheese, jam, chocolate milk

Weight Lifting Day
Chicken Breast w/ Brocolli

egg white, vegi omelet

Salsa, Tilapia, Tofu, Green Beans

Weight and Cardio
Protein Shake w/ Fruit

Sweet Potato w/ Greek Yogurt

Gasifier Diagrams:

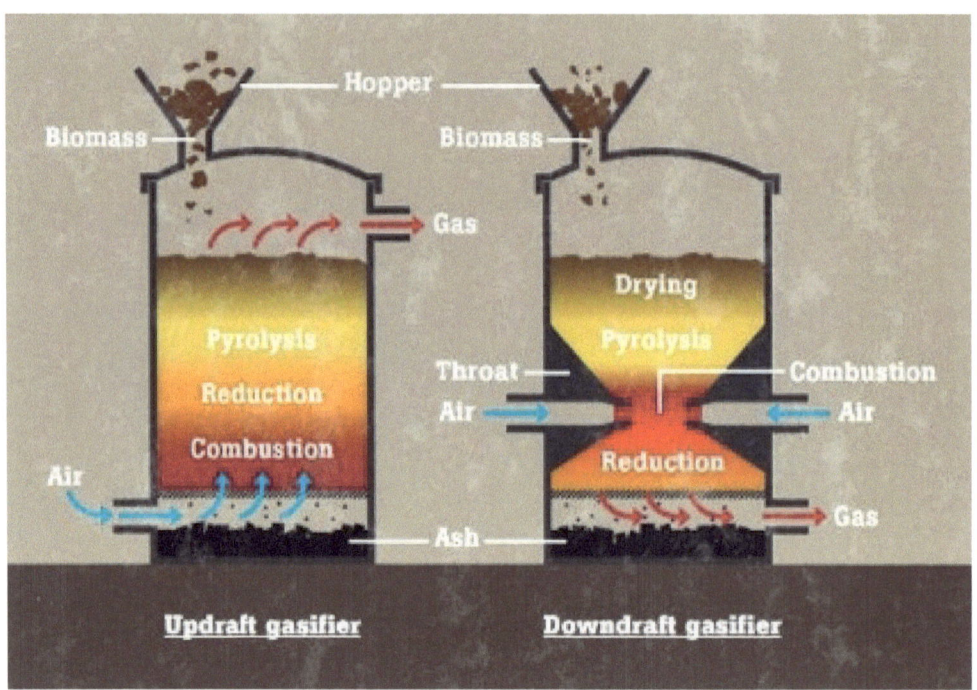

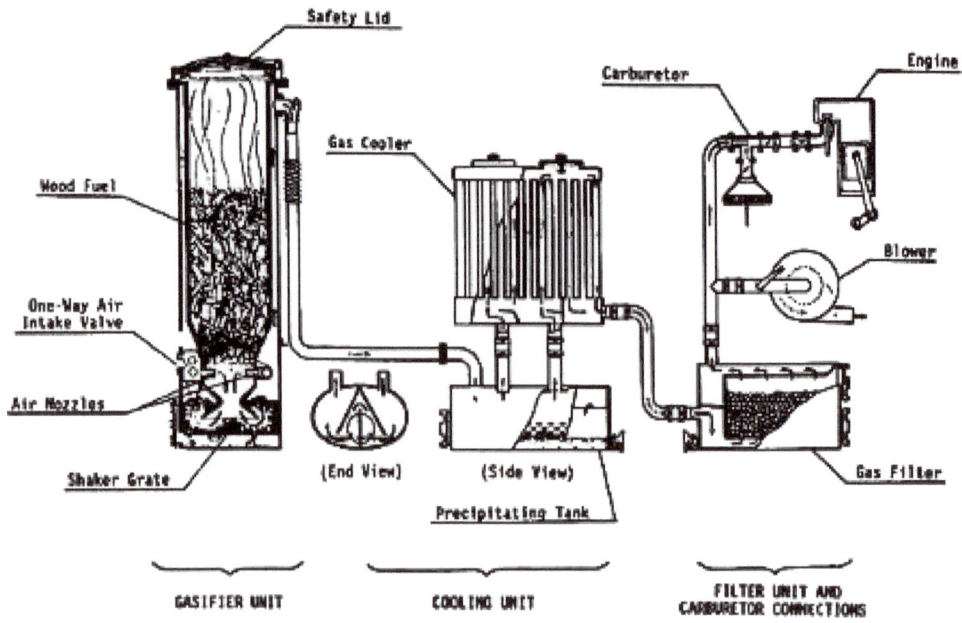

Rope Tying Diagrams:

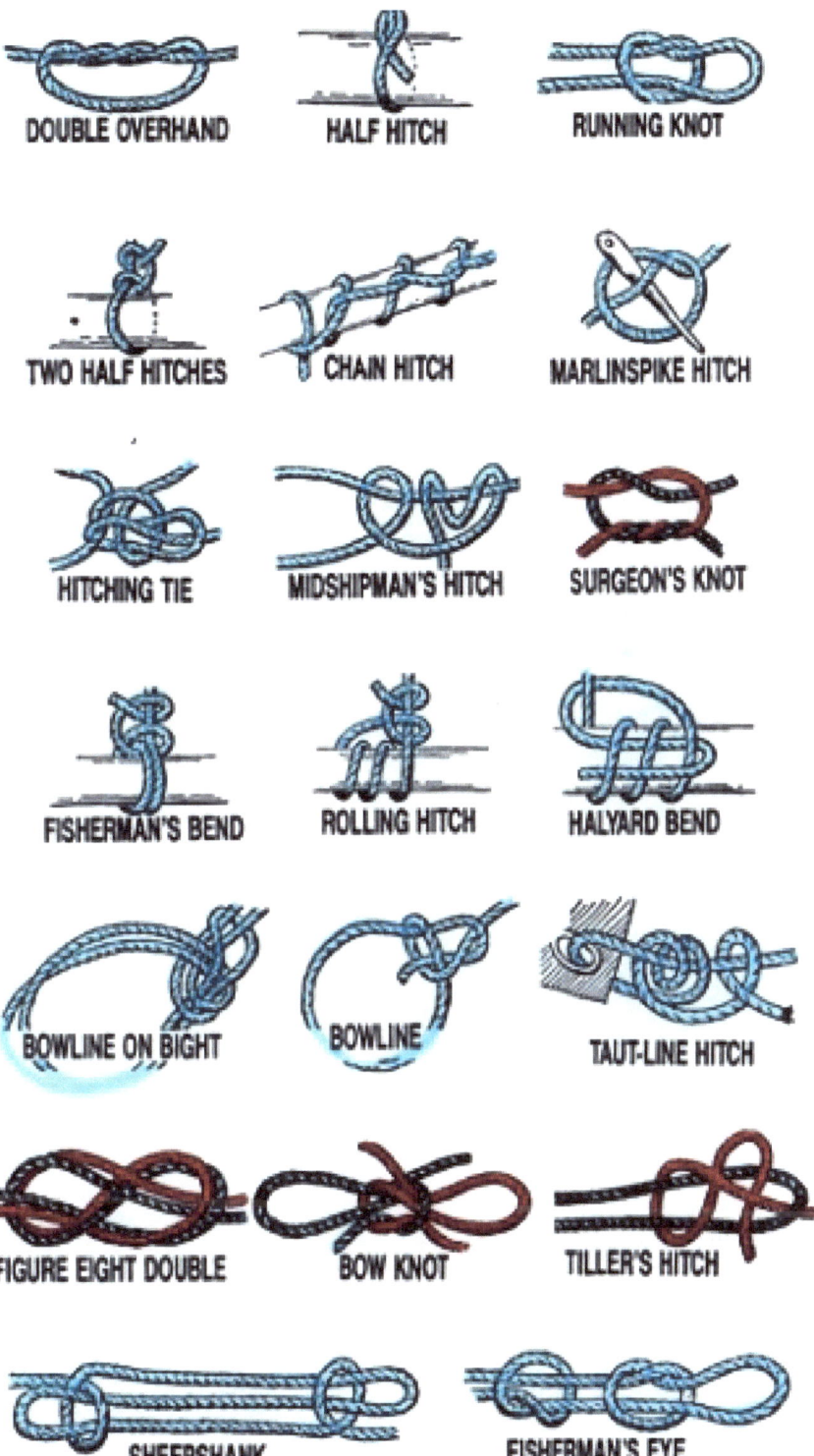

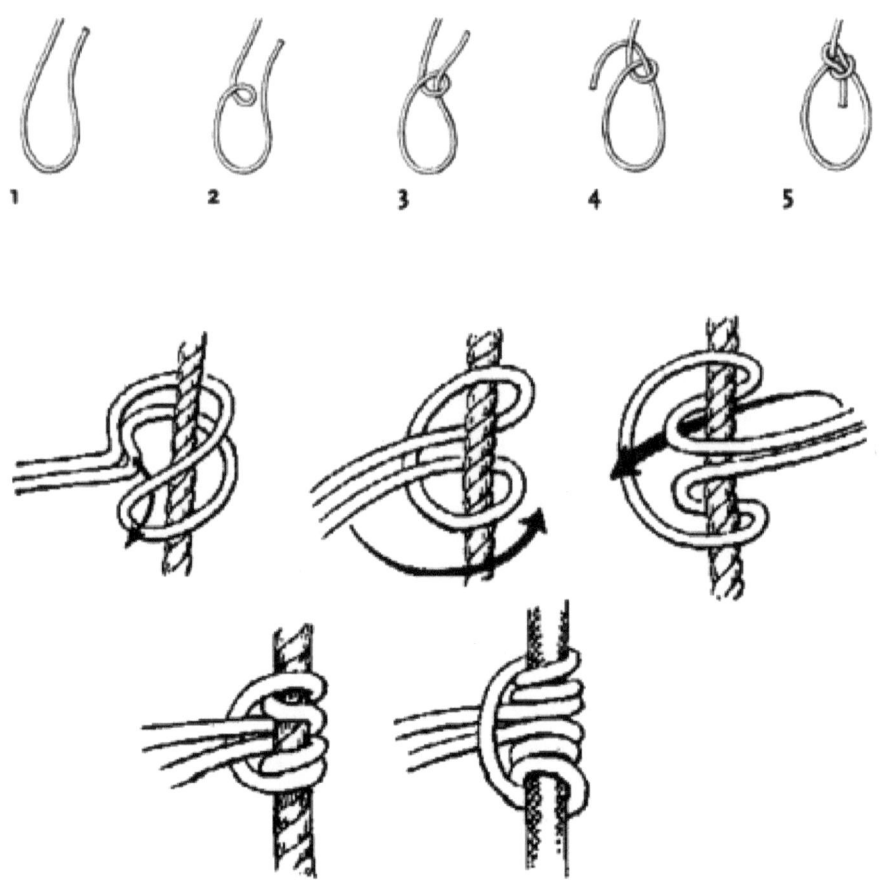

The End

www.ingramcontent.com/pod-product-compliance
Lightning Source LLC
Chambersburg PA
CBHW041458280526
45792CB00004B/1052